SPACE COLONY

Also by Franklyn M. Branley

Blacks Holes, White Dwarfs, and Superstars
Columbia & Beyond: The Story of the Space Shuttle
Comets, Meteoroids, and Asteroids: Mavericks of the Solar System
The Earth: Planet Number Three
The Electromagnetic Spectrum: Key to the Universe
Jupiter: King of the Gods, Giant of the Planets
Mars: Planet Number Four
The Milky Way: Galaxy Number One
The Moon: Earth's Natural Satellite
The Nine Planets
The Sun: Star Number One

alibris

TOP NOTCH BOOKS
8801 HWY. 377 W
TOLAR, TX 76476
UNITED STATES

To: ALIBRIS APEX DC 76670950-76
APEX
800 AVONDALE AVE.
GRANDVIEW HEIGHTS, OH 43212-3473

Shipping Instructions for TOPNOTCH

Print this Packing Slip and enclose inside the front cover of the book.

Please ship this item no later than Fri Aug 14, 2026.

Ship to:

ALIBRIS APEX DC 76670950-76
APEX
800 AVONDALE AVE.
GRANDVIEW HEIGHTS, OH 43212-3473
UNITED STATES

SPACE COLONY

FRONTIER OF THE 21st CENTURY

FRANKLYN M. BRANLEY

DIAGRAMS BY LEONARD D. DANK

Elsevier/Nelson Books
New York

THE ILLUSTRATIONS USED IN THIS BOOK HAVE BEEN SUPPLIED COURTESY OF THE FOLLOWING SOURCES:

NASA—pages vi, 9, 11, 15, 23, 34, 43, 45, 57, 67, 72, 84, 86, 88, 90
PIERRE MION © National Geographic Society—pages 17, 47
DON DIXON—pages 50, 54, 91, 94
BOEING AEROSPACE COMPANY—pages 53, 63, 66

Library of Congress Cataloging in Publication Data

Branley, Franklyn Mansfield.
Space colony: frontier of the 21st century.
Bibliography: p.
Includes index.
1. Space colonies. I. Title.
TL795.7.B7 1981 629.44′2 81-15294
ISBN 0-525-66741-5 AACR2

Published in the United States by E. P. Dutton, Inc., 2 Park Avenue, New York, N.Y. 10016. Published simultaneously in Canada by Clarke, Irwin & Company Limited, Toronto and Vancouver.
Editor: Virginia Buckley Designer: Trish Parcell
Printed in the U.S.A. First edition
10 9 8 7 6 5 4 3 2

Contents

The space shuttle will carry people and equipment to low-Earth orbit and then return to Earth. The fuel tanks on either side of the shuttle will detach and return to Earth by parachute. The large fuel tank (31 meters long and 8.5 meters across) will be modified in orbit and used as a habitat in space and on the Moon.

1

From Florida to Colony Two

In the twenty-first century colonies will be built thousands of kilometers from Earth, and great numbers of people will live and work in them. Parts of the colonies will be work areas and other parts will be habitats, places where people will live. The colonists will communicate with Earth via videophone. They will also send back radio-letters such as this:

January 2067
Colony Two

Dear Peggy and Arthur:

Jenny and I have been in Colony Two for twenty-four hours now. I'll start this note while our impressions are still fresh.

The space terminal in Florida was familiar ground to us because of the weeks we had spent there during the training period late last year. We met some of the people from our class who would be with us in the same shuttle flight. After the final medical checks and weigh-in, we went to the locker rooms where we removed our clothing. We had to shower thoroughly and wash our hair to get as clean as possible. Then we dressed in colony clothing, which is sterilized. It is also lightweight and very comfortable.

When we got to the waiting room, we could see the shuttle, a larger version of the first shuttles that were used in the 1980's. Crew members were checking the fueling. After a while all 150 of us went aboard. We stretched out in our bunks and fastened the belts.

Lift-off went smoothly. All we felt was a slight push on the bunk. They say the force was about three times gravity, but it didn't feel that way.

Soon there was no gravity, and we were weightless. It's a strange feeling, but we didn't get sick—although some people surely did. Fortunately for them, the flight was over in only half an hour. First thing we knew there was a slight bump, and we were at the zero-gravity section of Station One, which is in low-Earth orbit. A hostess from the station came floating in and helped us move out of the shuttle; we had to hold on, go from strap to strap, or we would float free.

From the docking area we went directly to the main part of Station One. What a surprise! There must have been a thousand people there, all waiting to go to Colony Two. Most of them were from the United States, but many came from all over the world. For two days we stayed in a hotel while more people gathered, two thousand altogether.

All of us were to go to Colony Two in the same ship. When the ship moved in to Station One, we watched it on closed-circuit television. It was huge—it seemed to be miles long. What made it so big was the long mass-driver engine and the solar cells that supply the power. The mass-driver is really a simple machine. It throws out pellets of lunar slag. As they are ejected, the ship moves in the opposite direction. Very little force is needed to make it move.

It took a long time for the whole length of the engine to go by. Finally the ship itself came into sight. It was a big ball with no windows at all—looking a bit like the head and tail of a tadpole. The sphere that held the people was so large you didn't even think of it as a ship—it seemed like a whole colony in itself, a moving colony. It took at least three hours for all of us to get aboard and find our cabins.

To protect its passengers against cosmic rays, there were no windows in the ship. But wherever you looked there were large video screens whose pictures were constantly changing from scans of the ship to views of Station One and Earth beyond.

We kept ourselves busy during the flight to Colony Two. Jenny and I joined classes to improve our 800-word basic Russian and Japanese. We were helped along because at dinner we were seated with colonists from those countries. We also made friends with people from China and Italy, and with others from many different parts of the world. We met an interesting Japanese couple upon our arrival at Station Two this morning. They are going to work on solar-power plants, just as we will. The woman is an agriculture specialist, and she has been telling us how the Japanese get so much food from small plots of land. I have to admit, though, that her English is a great deal better than my basic Japanese. I'll never catch on to some of those sounds.

We passed a power station on our first day. It was strange to see such a large structure "hanging" in space. Every now and then we see bright glints from other stations at various distances.

I guess the most exciting part of the journey was our first sighting of Colony Two. It wasn't spectacular, just a small bright spot in the black sky. But knowing this was to be our home made it all very exciting. As we got closer, details could be seen—the size of it was overwhelming. Our ship was big, but Colony Two is simply stupendous. Soon there will be at least ten thousand people here. No doubt both of us are going to be very busy—there is so much to be done.

By the time you receive this, sometime tomorrow, we'll have lots more to tell you. We'll call you on the videophone next week, so you can see us in our new home, and we can see how all of you are.

Love,
Jenny and Tom

2

Functions and Locations of Space Colonies

Many people are convinced that space colonies will be in our future. Already several universities, engineering societies, and the federal government have spent large sums of money to explore many of the problems that must be solved. Most experts agree that it is possible to build such colonies.

The first space colonies will be close to Earth and revolve around us, just as the Moon and man-made satellites do. Later they will be at other locations, perhaps in Earth orbits farther out, or even in the asteroid belt between the orbits of Mars and Jupiter. And colonies may eventually be built in much more remote parts of the solar system, or even beyond it.

Functions of Space Colonies

The location of a colony will depend largely upon its purpose—for example, the construction of solar-power satellites. These will be large installations designed to convert solar energy into electricity, which will then be sent to Earth. Many engineers believe that several such satellites will furnish enough electricity to provide the whole Earth with all the power it will need—reason enough to build a space colony. These power stations are being planned to be built 36 000 kilometers from Earth. At that distance they will always be above the same region—they will be in geosynchronous orbit, an orbit "in time" or "in step" with the Earth.

Other colonies, much closer to Earth, might manufacture certain small light products that will be sent to Earth upon completion. It has been argued that this will be expensive. Why not make the products on Earth in the first place? The answer is that there is zero gravity (weightlessness) in space, as well as an almost perfect vacuum (absence of air and impurities). Under zero gravity, mixtures are homogeneous, which means they are exactly the same throughout. Suppose you made a mixture of soil and water and let it stand for a while. The densest particles in the soil would sink to the bottom; the least dense would settle at the top. In outer space, the particles in such a mixture do not separate. The mixture remains unchanged.

Under such conditions it is possible to grow perfect crystals. Crystals of various substances, such as quartz, hematite, or tourmaline, grow in a solution, just as salt crystals grow in a salt-and-water solution. In space, the solution is homogeneous, so the crystals have no variations in them. Crystals are used to control electric circuits, to generate small amounts of electricity, and to measure currents; they are used widely in the electronics industry. The more perfect and uniform throughout the crystals are, the better they function.

The production of powerful and long-lasting magnets is also related to crystal growing. In space the molecules in a piece of metal can be precisely controlled, which means they can be lined up to produce a strong magnetic field. Magnets from a space factory will be greatly superior to the best magnets on Earth.

Colonies in low-Earth orbits will be able to manufacture perfect glass—of the same composition throughout. This glass will be used to make flawless lenses for all kinds of optical work.

Other colonies close to Earth might repair satellites. At this moment more than a thousand satellites are going around the Earth. They are photographing Earth, relaying telephone messages and television from continent to continent, gathering weather data, surveying military installations. Although built to last a long time, these satellites may be hit by particles in space, or they may suffer equipment breakdowns. If this happens, the satellite becomes a complete loss. Crews aboard space colonies will pick up such ailing satellites, make the necessary repairs, and place them back in orbit. Some colonies will manufacture and launch new satellites.

There are many more functions for space colonies, some of which will be discussed later. All those mentioned here are related to Earth, their purpose being to support Earth's people and industries.

In time, space colonies will become independent

of Earth. They will be self-sufficient—able to provide all the air, water, food, and energy necessary to sustain life. People will be born in space colonies and will spend their entire lives in them, leaving only for brief holiday excursions. They will monitor space, hoping to receive some indication that there are other civilizations in our galaxy. Sensitive radio receivers will be aimed at other star systems. Eventually, a space colony may be launched into a wide-sweeping orbit that may take the colonists beyond the Sun and outside the solar system on a journey to the distant stars.

Before engineers could think realistically about space colonies, there had to be some way of getting heavy materials into space at a reasonable cost. This became possible with the development of the space shuttle, the workhorse of the space age. Space colonies are no longer idle dreams. Far-seeing engineers involved in the project have already worked out many of the details, such as the size and shape of space colonies, how they will be built, and the way people will live on them.

Locations of Colonies

Many people believe it would be more sensible to build a colony on the Moon instead of in space. The Moon has a landing surface, solid ground underfoot, plenty of sunshine, and vast amounts of valuable minerals. Or, they say, if not on the Moon, the colony should be built on Mars. The temperature there is not impossibly cold. And the planet has smooth, rolling areas that would be good for landing and for erecting buildings.

Scientists have many reasons for believing that colonies should not be built on the Moon, on Mars, or on any other planet. The main reason is that the Moon and the planets all have gravity. A tremendous amount of fuel is needed to launch a spaceship from Earth because the force of gravity must be overcome.

We can imagine gravity as a deep hole out of which a rocket must climb. When a rocket takes off from Earth, the hole is a very deep one because Earth's gravity is strong. The gravity of the Moon is weaker, and so the "gravity hole" is not as deep. The gravity of Mars is less than half Earth's gravity, so the hole there is less than half as deep. Even so, it takes a lot of fuel for rockets to take off from either Mars or the Moon. The fuel cost for launching dozens of ships from a settlement on the Moon or Mars would be much too high to make the colony worthwhile. Also, if a colony were built on the Moon or Mars, many of the benefits of space itself would be lost. One of these benefits is weightlessness.

The gravity of a body—Earth, for example—depends on its mass—the amount of material in it. The mass of Earth is 6 000 000 000 000 000 000 000 (6 sextillion) metric tons. Its gravity, let us say, is 1. The mass of the Moon produces a gravitation that is one-sixth Earth's. The mass of Mars produces a gravitation that is four-tenths that of Earth. The gravity hole of the Moon (out of which ships have to climb) is therefore one-sixth as deep as Earth's; that of Mars is four-tenths as deep.

The mass of a satellite such as Skylab, the large space laboratory that was launched in the early 1970's, was a tiny fraction of Earth's mass. As a result, its gravity was very

Ships will use rockets that burn chemical fuel for landing on the Moon (and eventually on asteroids) and for leaving the surface. They will move from lunar orbit to the Moon surface.

small; in fact, it was close to zero. Rockets taking off from Skylab had no hole to climb out of; the slightest push was enough to get the rocket launched.

A space colony will have a low mass also—it will contain a very small amount of material as compared to the Moon or a planet. That means it will have very little gravity, and rockets can take off from it easily.

Equally important, rockets can dock at the colony easily. When a space vehicle lands on the Moon, retro-rockets (rockets that fire backward) aboard the vehicle must be fired to keep it from crashing into the surface as it is pulled down by the Moon's gravity. This must also be done when ships land on the Earth or on Mars. (Parachutes can also be used for landing on those planets that have dense enough atmospheres to support them.) Since a colony in space has essentially no gravity, so that spaceships are not pulled to it, the ships can move in very slowly, or pass by without great interference. Very little power is needed to dock there, or to take off.

Building in Space

Materials for the early colonies will have to be carried into space from Earth. The entire structure will be built on Earth, then taken down and transported on shuttles to an assembling area in space. Individual sections will consist of metal sheets and girders small enough to fit into the cargo area of a shuttle.

After each shuttle goes into orbit, its cargo is unloaded. The various parts are lifted out, and each part continues in the same orbit as the shuttle. Tethers keep the sections from separating, as they might if they were struck by meteoroids or by massive showers of particles from the Sun. After scores of round trips by the shuttles, the various units of the structure will be in orbit. Then assembly can begin.

A shuttle orbiter with engineers and a construction crew aboard rendezvous with the girders and other sections. Men

Tremendous structures can be assembled in space. Here a space shuttle moves in with supplies. Engineers assemble an array of solar mirrors that heat gases inside the long tube. These hot gases will drive electric turbines, shown just beyond the shuttle.

and women in space suits enter an air lock in the shuttle and then go into space. Small jets on backpacks enable them to move about and bring the sections together. Since everything is weightless, the slightest jet-force will move the pieces. Once in contact, girders are welded by detonating charges built into them. The intense heat that develops "melts" the girders together. Gradually, girders grow into subassemblies, and these are joined to make larger units.

Many of the basic operations, such as welding girders,

may be done by automatic assemblers. These will be computer controlled. The assembler will be directed by the computer to move a girder into position and to set off the charge that will complete a weld. Machines that do tasks similar to this are now used on Earth. For example, wings for Jet Liners are assembled and riveted by computer-controlled machines.

Thus the colony takes shape. Working in space takes considerable skill and practice. A space mechanic could start spinning if the jets were misfired, or a person might place himself in a trajectory that would continue away from the shuttle. Tethers fastened to the shuttle must be used by beginners to avoid such mishaps. But more experienced constructors will not need the restraints of a lifeline.

The first units will be only large enough to provide living space for a few engineers and technicians, besides containing equipment for obtaining useful metals and minerals from lunar soil and rocks. The first large colony, one that will contain thousands of settlers, will be about 320 000 kilometers from Earth at its farthest point and 160 000 kilometers at its closest. It will take about two weeks to go once around the Earth. The Moon is a bit farther out, some 384 000 kilometers away. Work crews will land on the Moon long before Colony Two is constructed. Some members of the crews will be construction engineers, others solar-electric specialists, and still others will be Moon miners.

3

The Space Colony

Space colonies will be huge structures, with towns and villages, theaters, schools, libraries, recreation areas, factories, farms for growing fruits and vegetables and for raising fish and small animals. A colony will have a steady supply of air, water, food and energy. All materials will be recycled over and over again, just as we are recycling metals, paper, and other materials in many places on our planet.

A colony will be completely sealed; otherwise, air and water could escape into space. (They would escape from Earth, too, if it were not for the strong gravity that holds them down.)

What will be the best "container" for the people in a colony—and all the farms, homes, schools, and factories they will need? Will it be a box, a hollow sphere, a cylinder? At this time the best shape has not yet been determined. In fact, there may not be a single "best" shape. Engineers may find that colonies can be built in a variety of forms. Perhaps space colonies will differ from one another.

One of the possibilities that engineers are looking into is a wheel-shaped colony—a wheel with six spokes and with a rounded "tire," called a *torus*.

The diameter of the wheel will be about 1800 meters, a bit over a mile. Some ten thousand people will live and work in the "tire" of the wheel, a tube 130 meters across. Six hollow cylinders (spokes of the wheel) will connect the tire to the central hub. Docks for spaceships arriving at and leaving the colony will be in the hub section.

Several other plans for colonies have been suggested. Many of the basic ideas for them originated almost a hundred years ago. In 1890 Konstantin Tsiolkovski, a Russian space pioneer, expressed an idea to be developed in a novel called *Beyond the Planet Earth:* "Humanity will not remain forever upon the Earth, but, in search of energy and room, will at first timidly venture beyond the edge of the atmosphere and then boldly move out and occupy all the worlds and spaces around the sun." Today many Russians still believe as Tsiolkovski did, and they are moving ahead in space exploration.

In the United States, present-day thinking about space colonies was first largely stimulated in the 1970's by Gerard K. O'Neill, a professor at Princeton University. He and his students decided to design a space colony and to explore the

A torus colony will be 1800 meters across. The long tube below the colony leads to a space factory. The large mirror reflects sunlight onto solar cells that produce electricity. The rings of mirrors around the center reflect sunlight into the habitat and farming areas inside the "tire."

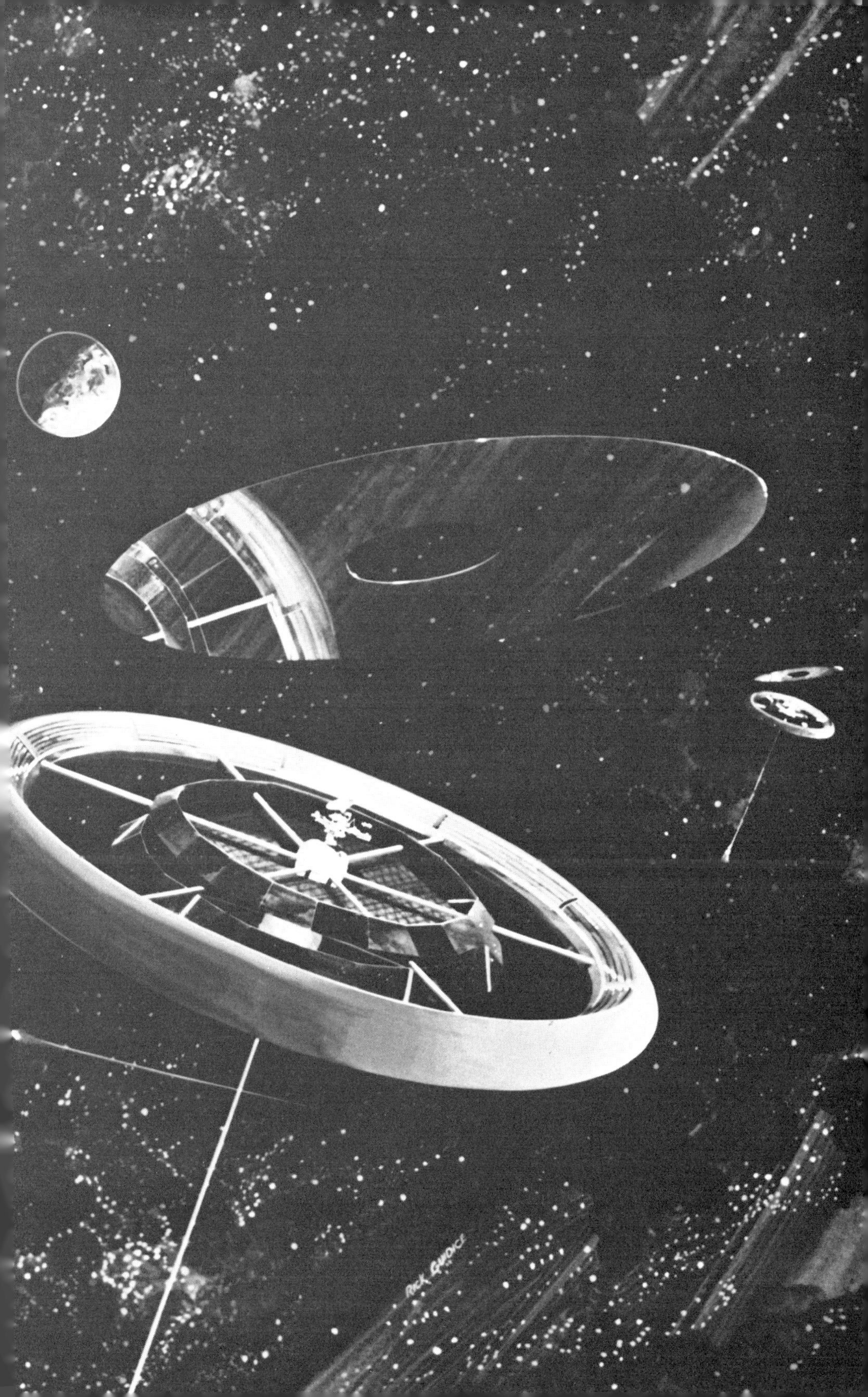
RICK GUIDICE

problems associated with it. They studied the history of the subject and came up with details of colonies of different shapes and sizes, including the torus. One of their plans was simply a large sphere. Another idea proposed was to stretch the sphere to make a tube rounded at the ends. Such a design may eventually be used; it may even be the shape of the first colony. Further studies will be made to determine which colony design is best. Later in this book we'll look at the stretched-sphere colony.

Let's begin though by considering the rotating wheel—the torus colony. This proposal was first suggested in 1929, but few people heard about it. In the 1950's Wernher von Braun spread the idea widely in a popular book called *Across the Space Frontier*. In it he gave details of a wheel-shaped colony. In the 1970's engineers carried the wheel idea further.

The colony will be built out of aluminum sheets and girders. Construction will begin with the hub, for that is where ships will dock. One or two spokes will then be erected. Sections of the torus will be connected to the ends of the spokes. As soon as this much has been completed, people will begin to live inside the sections, and crops will be planted. A flat array of solar cells built around the hub will provide electric power to the hub, and to engineers constructing the other torus sections. As a second section is completed, it will be eased into contact with a spoke. This section will then be connected to the first section, which is already in position. And so the task will continue until all six sections have been linked together to make the torus complete.

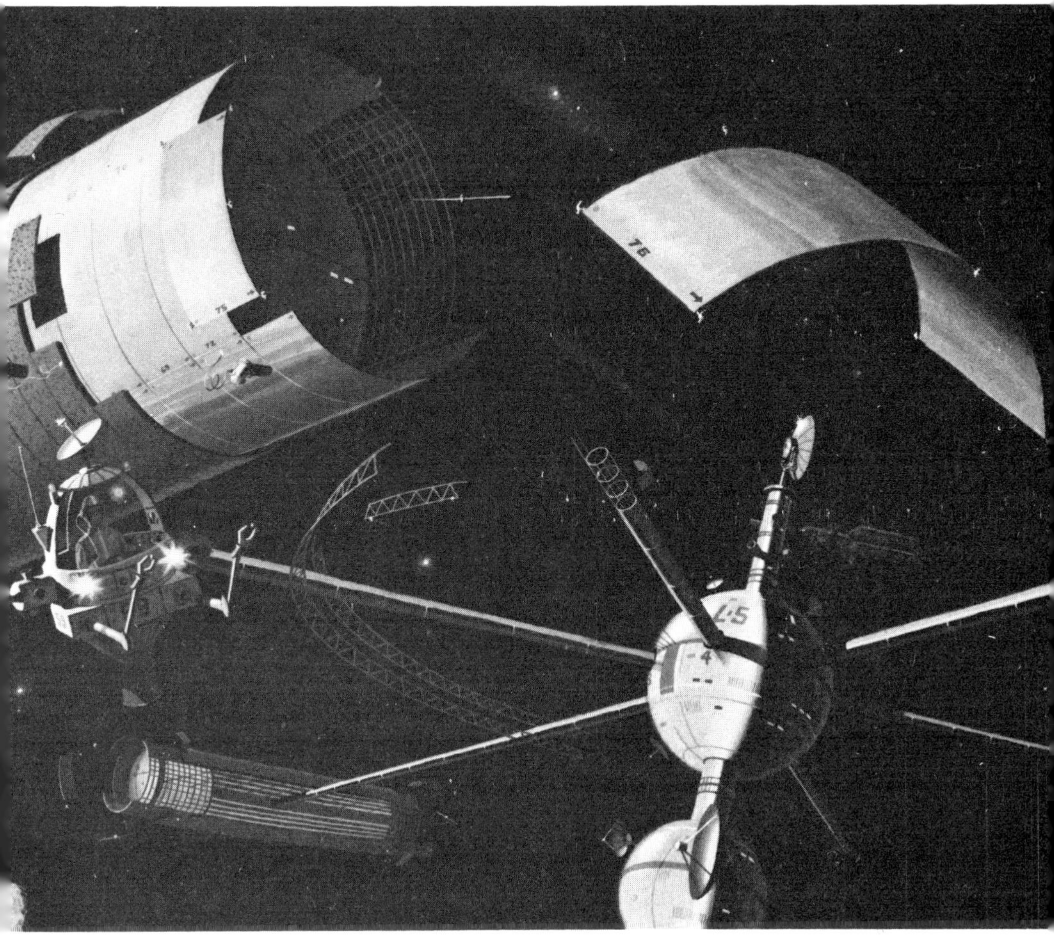

A space colony takes shape. Central hub at lower right has been completed, and a section of the torus is in place at lower left. Another section is being assembled at upper left. Slabs of lunar insulating material cover part of it. An engineer in an assembly tug moves sections together by manipulating small jets.

Eventually the entire torus will be covered with sheets of slag, left over from the removal of metal ores from lunar soil. (Many of the materials for the colony will come from the

Moon, as explained in Chapter 5.) The slag will insulate the torus from cosmic rays. The hub and spokes will be only partially protected, for people will not be in them for long periods of time.

Cosmic rays, of which there are many in outer space, are made of high-energy particles. The primary particles, which are bits and pieces of atoms, are very powerful and move at high speeds. They have so much energy that they will produce high-energy X rays if they strike a colony. To avoid being bombarded, the colony will have to be shielded. This will call for many tons of lunar slag. Fortunately, lunar slag will be available as a by-product. It will provide very effective protection. Secondary particles, which contain less energy, strike us here on Earth all the time. But they pass through us, with no ill effects so far as we know.

Slag shielding cannot go all around the torus, for one-third of it must be windows to admit sunlight. The windows will be screened with a series of V-shaped aluminum strips set on their edges. The strips will be spaced so that before particles can enter the torus, they must strike aluminum surfaces four times. In this way, the particles will lose much of their energy, thus greatly reducing the danger to the colonists.

The aluminum surfaces will also reflect sunlight, which will penetrate into the torus; it will be available twenty-four hours a day. Agricultural areas will use the sunlight almost continuously to speed crop growth. In the residential areas, and also in some of the farming regions, sunlight will be reduced in the evening to produce the regular day-night cycle, a rhythm that is beneficial to many plants and animals, and certainly to humans. Variation in sunlight may be obtained by tilting the shields, or by tilting mirrors, as will be explained later.

The remaining two-thirds of the torus will be surrounded by the cosmic-ray shield of lunar slag. This will not be fastened to the torus. The colony will turn inside the slag shield.

The Completed Colony

The "tire" of the colony will have areas for living and for farming, as well as for schools, stores, public buildings, and theaters. The spokes will contain elevators for moving people and supplies back and forth between the hub and the torus. They will also contain electric cables and heat-exchange pipes. These pipes will be connected to a large flat radiator outside the colony. More heat than is desirable will build up in the colony, and it will have to be removed. The radiator will do this. Temperature will be kept at a fairly even range between 18 and 22 degrees Celsius.

The torus and the spokes will rotate slowly, making one complete rotation every minute. The central hub will also rotate; however, the docking portion of the hub will not. Rotation of the "wheel" produces a centrifugal force, which "throws" objects away from the axis—the hub. The force acts like gravity on the people in the torus. Gravity pulls them away from the hub. As they move through the spokes toward the hub, this gravity will decrease.

At the hub there will be zero gravity. A small hospital in the hub will care for patients who are more comfortable under zero gravity—heart patients and patients with breathing problems or problems related to movements of the legs and arms.

A large mirror a mile or so across made of many small mirrors fastened together will be positioned above the hub. The mirror will be angled so sunlight falls on it twenty-four hours a day. The sunlight will be reflected from the mirror onto plates of solar cells that generate electricity for the entire colony. Sunlight directed to two rings of movable mirrors fastened to the spokes will be directed through the windows of the torus into the interior.

The mirrors on these rings will be movable so they can be tilted to control the amount of sunlight for the different areas of the torus. Certain farming regions will require intense sunlight. Housing regions will need less sunlight, and they will also need a day-night cycle. In the evening, mirrors directed at housing areas will be tilted to produce twilight, followed by complete darkness—the mirror will reflect no sunlight into that section. Some areas of the torus will be having "sunrise" while others will be in "sunset." It will be possible to close off each of the six sections. At night a farming region may continue to receive light. By closing off the section, there will be no light-spill into the living area.

A long, hollow tube will extend 10 kilometers from the bottom of the hub. At the end of the tube (which is for transport) there will be an automated factory—perhaps a metal-processing plant that combines titanium with aluminum to make an extremely light but strong and hard alloy, one that because of gravity cannot be produced on Earth. The factory might also extract aluminum from lunar ore, although this task will usually be done at another location, called a construction shack. A panel of solar cells will be the "furnace" for the factory. Excess heat will be expelled through a cargo radiator similar to the one outside the colony itself. Engineers from the colony who will check the factory will go there through the long service tube.

Another large structure will also be part of the colony—the heat radiator already mentioned. Its edge will face the Sun, so that the flat surfaces are always dark. Excess heat from the torus is carried to the panel and the heat radiated into space. (In a similar fashion, heat radiates into space from Earth during the night hours.) By using the radiator, and by regulating solar intensity, the temperature inside the torus will be kept at a comfortable level.

Entering the Colony

When a transfer vehicle is sent to the colony from a low-Earth orbit, it must first achieve a new orbit, one that matches that of the colony. Considerable power will be needed to do this, because the colony will be much farther away from Earth than the location of the station in low-Earth orbit. The vehicle will move from an orbit that is close to Earth—some 250 kilometers away—to one that is much farther out, perhaps 320 000 kilometers. Once the colony's orbit has been matched, little fuel is needed, for the transfer vehicle can ease in closer and closer by using low-power engines. It will nose into a docking port in the hub of the colony, where it will be fastened.

Passengers will leave the vehicle and move into the narrow docking section. From there they will enter the central hub. This will be a large sphere, 130 meters in diameter, and it will be turning slowly. The people will still be in zero gravity, a condition they will have experienced during much of the voyage from the low-Earth location. It will be necessary for them to use straps and handholds to keep from floating free.

The six spokes that radiate from the central hub connect to the six sections of the torus, three for residential areas and three for farming sections. As the new arrivals to the torus move in elevators outward from the hub, they feel "gravitation." Weightlessness ends gradually. People feel the floor pushing under their feet, and they are able to move about without using the straps and handholds needed when weightless. The elevator moves slowly, for the change from weightlessness to gravity is made over a distance of only one kilometer. Too quick a change could cause people to become nauseous.

Moving out of the elevator into the torus, the new arrivals are struck by the bright sunlight that shines into the torus. They see trees, plants and flowers all about them.

Nearby there are buildings, houses, and apartments of different sizes. Some of them are at "ground" level, whereas others are built along the sides of the torus at levels that rise like houses built on a hillside. Each of the residential segments can house about 3,500 people, who will come from many different countries.

Perhaps the most important attribute of a space colonist will be a spirit of adventure, a desire to make a new world. All colonists will also need to have specialized training and skills in engineering, construction, farming, or electronics that can be used for the good of the colony.

Homes and apartments will be placed in a parklike setting. Sunlight will be controlled to give a day-night cycle.

Streets in the torus are short, and they curve occasionally to add interest. Schools, offices, libraries, hospitals, and community centers are found at various levels also. Food stores, as well as variety shops—clothing, gifts, stationery, books—tend to be on the "ground" level. By building "upward" an open feeling is preserved, so that even though there may be ten thousand people in the colony, there is no crowded feeling. In the far distance, the buildings curve upward and blend into greenery, a farming segment. The residential areas alternate with the farming sections.

No electronic or telephone wires can be seen strung from place to place. These and all water pipes, air-regulating controls, and waste areas are placed beneath "ground" level. Transportation is mostly by foot, for distances are not great; the farthest houses are only about 400 meters from an elevator. For the most part, homes and apartments are close to an elevator spoke, so people will be able to use the elevator to move from one section of the torus to another should they wish to. However, in order to do this they would have to go from maximum gravity (in the torus) to zero gravity (in the hub), and then back again to maximum gravity. Although such a change is not harmful to the body, many people could become nauseous, "travel sick."

To avoid this, and to ease movement of bulky supplies from one part of the torus to another, a monorail car runs around the torus. To conserve space, the train runs on a rail suspended from the inner part of the torus, the "top" from the standpoint of the settlers.

Apartments vary in size, and the decor reflects the taste of individual tenants. Regardless of size, each has a front balcony or deck. And just about every balcony has large built-in boxes for growing flowers and small vegetables. From the balcony, settlers can see flowers all about them and trees and garden areas along the streets, giving them a feeling of the outdoors.

Clever variations in the buildings hide the fact that they are built of modules—prefabricated sections. Columns and girders for the structures are solid aluminum and floors are made of panels about 5 centimeters thick. They will be "sandwiches," with aluminum sheeting on the outside and spongelike aluminum between them. Walls are made of sheets of fiberglass. Many are colorless, but others have colors and designs built into them. The size of apartments and their layout are flexible, depending upon family needs and individual preferences. Wood and plastics are virtually nonexistent, for they must be brought from Earth. Furniture and fittings are mainly of metal or glass, since these can be made from materials found in lunar soil.

Most people will rent their apartments, though a few will be owned by the occupants. When the colonists arrive they will make monthly payments to the government, and so their monthly "rents" will pay off the mortgage. For the most part these "owners" will have decided to spend their lives and rear their children in the colony.

Government will be determined by the colonists, except in matters concerning security. Perhaps three people from each of the living segments will make up a council, with a chairman who serves for one year to be chosen from among those nine. The council may be responsible for education, business permits, parks and playgrounds, and transportation systems.

Superior to the council will be the security officer. An entire colony could be wiped out be a small group, or even an individual, simply by puncturing the shell in many locations, by disrupting the power supply to the ventilation and recycling systems, or by introducing a herbicide (a chemical that kills vegetation) to the garden areas. The security officer and his or her aides will be responsible for preventing any kind of sabotage, for making immediate repairs, and for deciding which problems warrant attention first.

Sensors of various kinds will be located throughout the colony, constantly feeding information to the center about air composition and pressure, water flow, humidity, the growth of crops, by-products of waste recycling, the intensity of cosmic particles, the amount of sunlight received and the rhythm of sunlight and darkness. In most cases, variations in such factors will be adjusted by automatic controls. However, one person, probably assisted by two aides, will decide what action to take in an emergency and have the power to call upon any colonist to work on its correction.

4

Staying Alive in the Colony

In order to stay alive, each of us needs a constant supply of air, water, food, and heat. Earth is surrounded by a blanket of air. The supply appears endless, and so we are not usually concerned about it. The percentages of oxygen, nitrogen, and carbon dioxide in the air change very little from day to day and year to year. Humidity in the air (the amount of water vapor) goes up and down; so do the percentages of dust and pollution. Many pollutants from cars and factories enter the air, and they can cause considerable trouble—for instance, when they contribute to the development of smog, which occasionally settles over a region, or to acid rain, which can poison lakes, often killing the fish. Still, all the foreign particles in the air do not usually affect it enough to make it unsafe to breathe. It is constantly renewed by natural processes.

And so it is with water. In most places on Earth there is enough for everyone, and it is usually clean enough to be usable. All over the world, water becomes polluted by people, by wastes from factories and farms. But when the water evaporates, it leaves impurities behind. The water vapor then condenses and returns to Earth as rain or snow, which may pick up dust and ash. This natural cycle replenishes our water supply today just as it has been doing for millions of years.

As for food, in some places on Earth it is abundant, but there are many regions where it is in short supply. Actually, about two-thirds of the world's population is underfed, even though our planet is capable of producing enough food for everyone alive today. But the Earth does not produce a sufficient amount of food for a variety of reasons.

As crops draw minerals from the ground, the soil becomes exhausted, but it can be replenished by crop rotation, by "resting" it, or by using green fertilizer (planting a crop such as rye grass and digging it in to revitalize the soil).

The last essential ingredient for life is heat. Certain microbes can survive very high temperatures, whereas others can exist under sub-zero conditions. But most living things function best at temperatures that range between 15 and 20 degrees Celsius. In the daily day-night cycle, many places on Earth have average temperatures in this range. There are places that are much hotter, and others much colder, but Earth's mean temperature—the planetary temperature—stays at a constant 14 degrees Celsius. The amount of heat received from the Sun is balanced by heat loss through the atmosphere, and so the average temperature varies very little.

The essential requirements for life are the same in a space

colony as they are on Earth. There must be adequate amounts of air, water, food and heat.

Air

Whenever possible, the basic materials for our space colony will come from the Moon, for, as will be explained in Chapter 5, they will be less costly than they would be if transported from Earth. Oxygen for the atmosphere will be derived from lunar soil. Nitrogen, however, will have to come initially from Earth, as will the carbon for the carbon dioxide needed by plants for photosynthesis.

Atmospheric presssure in a space colony is about half of what it is on Earth. The lower pressure permits thinner walls in the colony, and a decreased amount of nitrogen in the air (about 57 percent). Some nitrogen is necessary to reduce fire hazards—things burn very rapidly in pure oxygen. Besides, plants can convert nitrogen to nitrates, water-soluble chemicals beneficial to growing things. About 40 percent of the atmosphere is oxygen; carbon dioxide amounts to slightly less than 1 percent, and about 2 percent is water vapor.

Animals and people inhale oxygen and exhale carbon dioxide, whereas plants primarily take in carbon dioxide and give off oxygen. Thus there must be a balance of these substances in the atmosphere of a space colony. Nevertheless, slight variations will develop. The atmosphere in our space colony is monitored constantly so that the proper amounts of the different gases are maintained.

There is some pollution, though it is not extreme, since

there are no gasoline or diesel engines and most factories are outside the colony. The most serious pollution comes from noxious gases given off by waste materials. These gases are absorbed by charcoal filters, whereupon the air is piped to a waste-treatment unit, where trace materials of other pollutants that it might contain are removed. This process is continuous. Energy requirements in the colony are minimal, and whatever power is needed comes from the solar-electric collectors.

Water

Large amounts of water will be needed for the farm sections and to carry off sewage, so farms will be designed to make full use of every drop. All the colonists must quickly learn to use water sparingly. Showers run intermittently, and the water used for them is recycled to "gray" water. "Gray" water is not as "white" (pure) as drinking water and goes directly to a farm segment. Only about two liters of water are needed to flush a toilet. (In most homes on Earth, toilets use 25– 30 liters of water.) Compressed air increases the sewage-carrying ability of the water. The sewage goes directly to waste-treatment plants for recycling.

The hydrogen in the water has to be brought from Earth; the oxygen comes from the Moon. Liquid water evaporates into the air from plants and animals, but the water vapor does not condense into clouds. The sky is always clear; it never rains in our colony. Although water vapor condenses on plants during the night, the standard procedure for turning gaseous water into liquid is to pass it through a condenser.

Once a colony has sufficient water for all the animals, plants, and people, there will be no need for replenishing the supply, since the water will be used over and over again. Wastes will be removed, drinking water purified. But water used by plants will remain gray water—though it will be partly purified, it will not be as pure as drinking water.

Food

If the colony is to be self-sufficient, many people will be involved in farming—planting and harvesting crops and caring for farm animals. For the most part, fruit will be grown in small plantings throughout the colony, and vegetables will be raised on patios and in park areas. Most of the food, however, will be grown in farm sections of the torus.

By closing off a farming zone, the farmers can use higher temperatures, if needed, and vary the amount of carbon dioxide in the air, and they can also control the humidity and the amount of light received—in short, adjust conditions to benefit the crops without affecting any other area.

A colony farm is built on four levels, which extend from the wall of the torus like shelves, one above the other. The upper level consists almost entirely of fish and rice ponds. Fish, which are rich in protein and grow rapidly, provide an important part of the colonists' diet. Water trickles from the ponds through filters to remove usable fish-food particles, and then to the level directly below. Wheat and other grains are the principal crops there.

Vegetables are grown on the level below the wheat. There is a good variety of them although protein-rich soybeans will take up the largest amount of space.

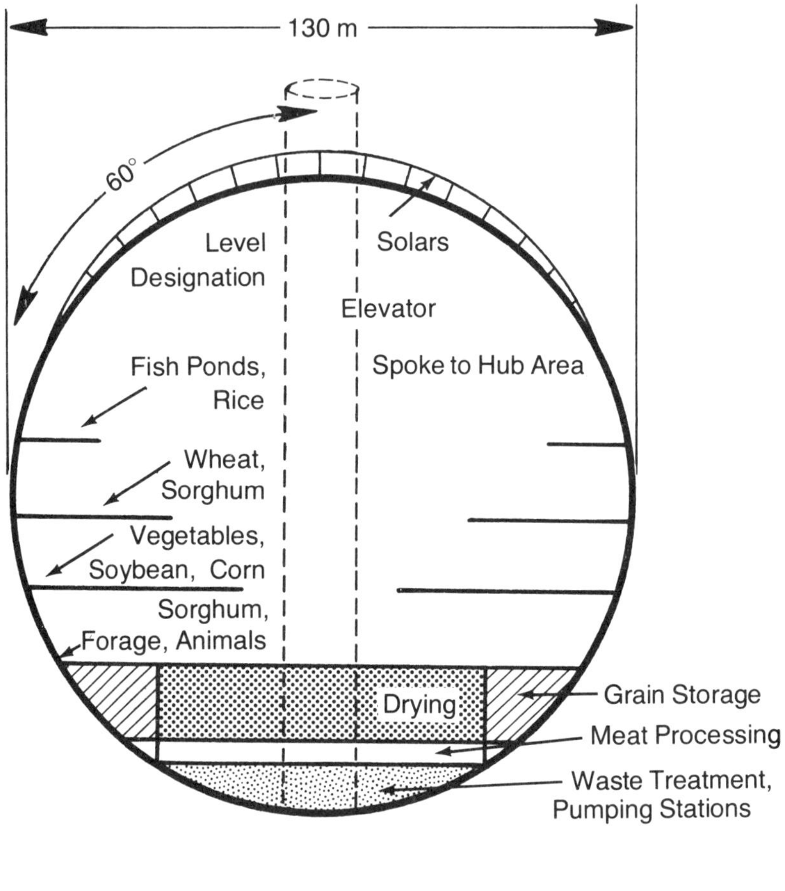

Diagram shows how the farming region in a space colony is built up in levels *(left).* Windows (solars) are located beneath aluminum "chevrons" *(right)* that prevent cosmic particles and meteoroids from striking them with full force.

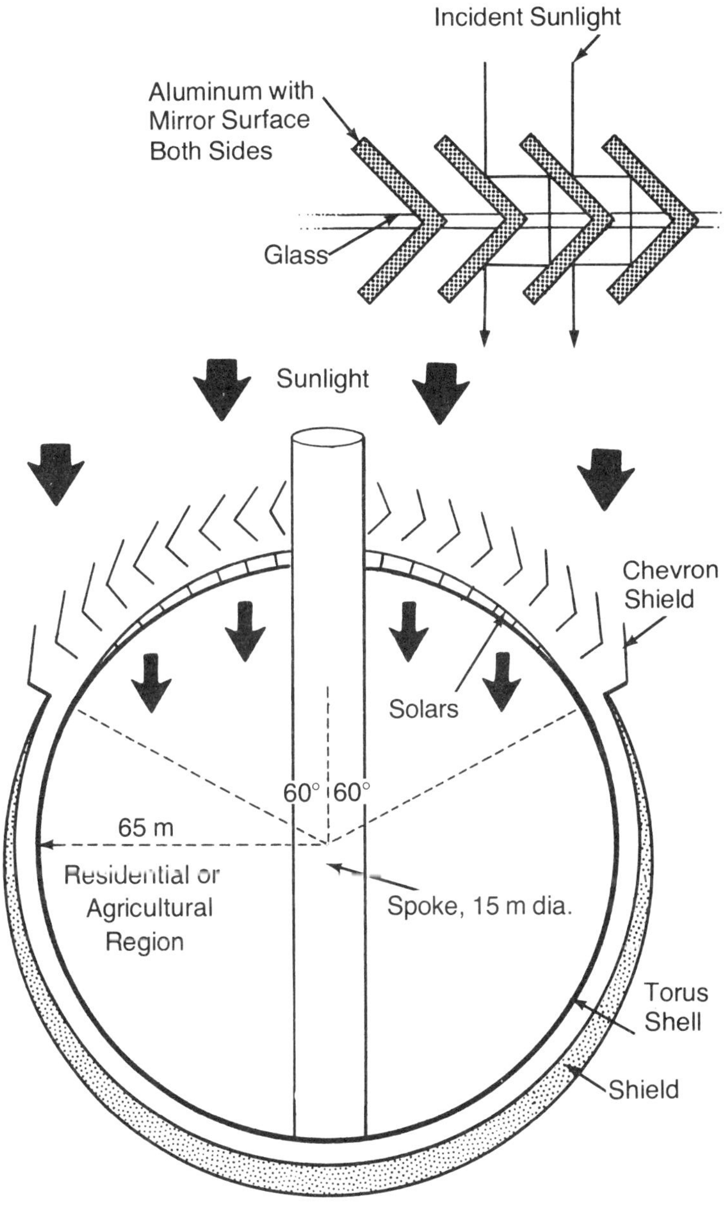

SHIELD AND CHEVRON CONFIGURATION

Farming sections will be built in terraces with different crops grown on each of the levels.

Below the vegetable level there is space for animals, and for crops for those animals to graze on. There are cows, but they are not used for meat; they supply milk and milk products. Meat comes from chicken and rabbits, animals that grow fast and require much less feed per pound of meat than cattle do.

Beneath this fourth level there are sections for drying and processing the food and getting it ready for delivery to the colonists. Water and waste must be recycled, and the equipment for doing this is also beneath the animal level.

Soil for the farms comes from the Moon. Lunar rocks are heated and then pulverized. Fertilizers, most of which are derived from lunar rocks, are trickled into the water. By adjusting the amount carefully, by regulating humidity and carbon dioxide, and by supplying sunshine for long periods, the farmers are able to produce large amounts of food from a small farming area. Yields may be ten times as great as those that can be achieved on Earth.

Heat

Since the colony will be in strong sunlight undiluted by a surrounding atmosphere, getting enough heat will be no problem. Heat builds up, however, so it must be gotten rid of as well as collected. Sunlight is reflected into the colony by movable mirrors. As the sunlight strikes solid surfaces within the colony, it is changed to heat. Thermostats open and close light filters to regulate the temperature—keep it from going too low or too high.

Heat is also given off by electrical equipment and by the plants and animals within the colony, so it does accumulate. To avoid this, pipes carry hot water or air from the interior to a radiator located outside the colony. This radiator has a broad surface containing a network of tubes, not unlike the radiator of a car. Its narrow edge faces the Sun, so it receives little or no heat, whereas its broad surface is exposed to the

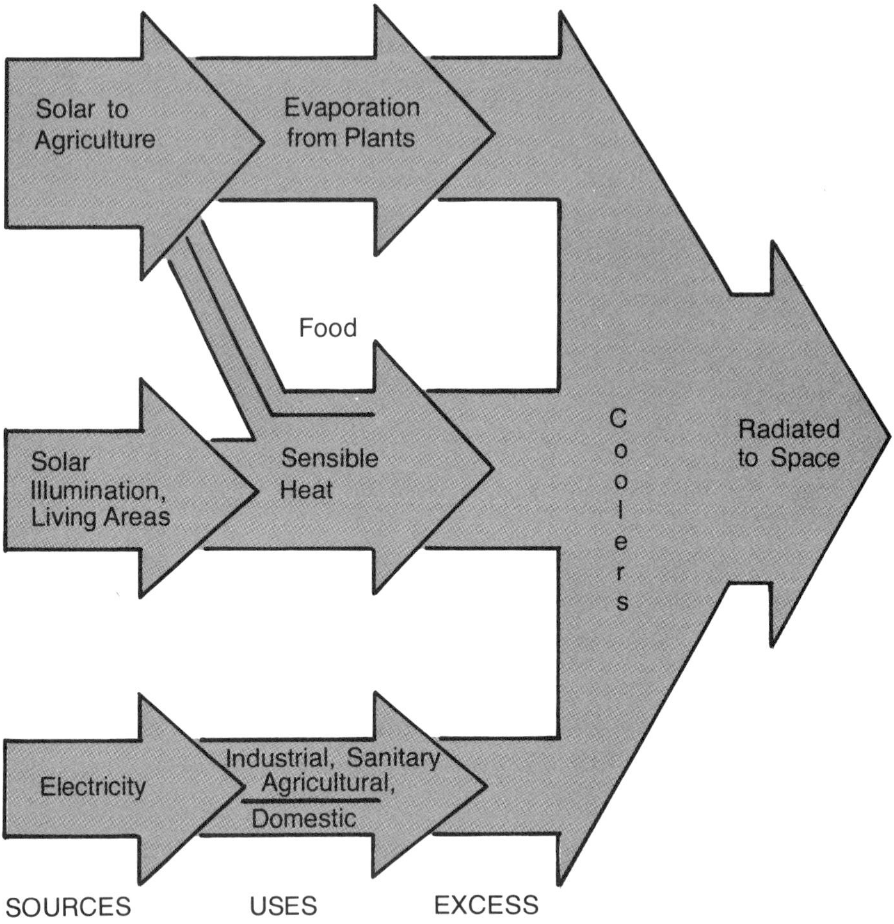

In a space colony heat is generated, used and then released. The chart shows sources of heat and how it is used. (Sensible heat means heat for comfort.) To keep a colony at an even temperature the heat released must equal heat input.

utter coldness of outer space. (Outer space is cold, but sunlight is intense. The sunlight becomes heat only when it strikes a surface.) In this way, heat passes from the radiator's broad surface to outer space, and the cooled air or water then circulates back into the colony. The entire colony is air-conditioned—kept at an even temperature—and the water vapor (humidity) maintained at a level that is comfortable for humans and animals and beneficial for plants.

Many colonists will probably find the uniform weather boring. In most places on Earth, weather is always changing. A rainy day has its delights, and so have wintry winds and snowstorms, clouds, and the succession of clear and gray days. Perhaps engineers will find they have to introduce changes into the colony's weather pattern—increase humidity so clouds develop and maybe even create a rain shower from time to time.

5

Moon Mining

The aluminum, iron, and other metals needed for building space colonies, as well as oxygen for the air and silica for glass, will come from the Moon. Before Colony Two is built, there will be a small space station in low-Earth orbit and two work stations on the Moon.

People will stay in a space station or a Moon station for only a few weeks or months. Then they will return to Earth. A station is different from a colony because it is only a temporary residence, whereas people in a space colony will spend their entire lives there, except for brief visits to the Earth, Moon, or other colonies.

Station in Low-Earth Orbit

The space station, which will have a twenty-four-member crew of specialists, will be located close to Earth, perhaps 250 kilometers away. The main part of the structure will be built from several large fuel tanks from space shuttles. The shuttles will also carry metal girders, beams, and life-support equipment (food, water, and air) to the low-Earth location. Once it has been assembled, the station will be occupied by the crew.

The shuttle fuel tanks are 31 meters long, and 8.5 meters in diameter. For living quarters, each tank is divided into several circular floor plans, with a ceiling height of 2.6 meters. Utilities and storage for each section are located in spaces underneath each floor. A central shaft 1.8 meters in diameter runs the entire length of each tank. This provides access to each of the sections.

Seven of the levels are each divided into three segments or apartments, for one or two persons. A level toward the center contains bath, toilet, and laundry facilities. The top double level has a domed ceiling and is a social center, a place for relaxing, games, and observation.

Communal tanks connected to the "living" tanks contain maintenance equipment —air and water purifiers, standby supplies, and sewage processors. Three levels are used for recreation—gymnasium, library, theater. Two levels are used for food storage, preparation and service; two other levels are for dining areas. The upper level is an area for moving in and out of the station. It contains space suits and oxygen supplies. An air lock with two doors, one to the station and the other to space, is built into the structure.

A person going to work outside the station puts on a space suit and goes into the air lock, closing both doors. Air in the lock is pumped out, pressure drops to zero. Then the engineer opens the door to space. Entering the station from space, the opposite procedure is followed. A person enters the air lock through the space-side door. Both doors are closed and air is admitted, bringing the pressure up to meet the inside pressure of the station. The engineer then opens the station-side door.

Residential tanks and communal tanks are fastened to two more tanks that contain equipment for controlling the environment throughout the station by supplying fresh water and the correct air mixture, reprocessing sewage and other wastes, and furnishing electricity. Food reserves are stored here, and some crops may be grown—fast-growing greens that do well in liquid culture.

Two identical clusters of residential, communal, and life-support tanks are joined to form a dumbbell-like structure. A tube 140 meters long connects them, as do cables to relieve strain in the tunnel. Halfway between the two clusters, the tunnel connects to a central hub. Shuttles from Earth will dock at this location. People and supplies from Earth will be delivered here through an air lock. People will remain at the station for only brief periods, so individuals will be returning regularly to Earth. They will reenter the shuttle through the hub.

The entire structure (the dumbbell) will make three rotations a minute. This will provide an artificial gravity throughout the tanks, as explained in Chapter 3.

Power for the station will come from large panels of solar cells. These will be very similar to the cells that have been used in various space satellites and planet probes since the 1960's. They are made of selenium crystals, which produce electricity when light falls upon them. Large panels 100 meters square will contain thousands of cells. They will be turned to receive sunlight continuously and so provide a steady supply of electricity.

Heat from people, lights, cooking, and sunlight will build up inside the station. Air will be circulated to pick up heat and carry it to a large radiator located outside the station. The radiator will be edge-on toward the Sun, so that its broad surfaces do not receive any sunlight. Heat in the air will be radiated into space, and the cool air returned to the station.

In the beginning there may be forty people aboard the station. Once all systems are in operation, the number will be reduced. The crew will follow a rigid work schedule, for there will be many jobs to be done. An important purpose of the station will be to make preparations for mining the Moon. It will be a staging area for readying payloads that will be put into orbit around the Moon. These payloads will include six shuttle tanks that will be landed there. Four of the tanks will be modified into habitats where the Moon miners will live. The other two tanks will become storage tanks for liquid fuel, to be used by rockets that will go back and forth between the lunar surface and lunar orbit.

Mass-Drive Engine

Chemical rockets will not be used for travel through space. Instead, the station will construct a mass-drive reaction engine that will be used to make round trips between the station and lunar orbit.

The engine will be made of electromagnets lining a long

hollow tube. Pellets of rock or metal are accelerated along the tube by the electromagnets and ejected from the engine. The force of the ejected particles causes the engine to move in the opposite direction. Electricity for the magnets is made by a panel of solar cells.

The action of the engine is somewhat like that of a sled on an ice-covered lake. Suppose you throw snowballs backward (the action). The sled will move forward because of reaction. It is the same principle as that used in a jet or a rocket engine: when hot gases are ejected, the jet (or rocket) moves in the opposite direction. In a similar fashion, a mass-driver engine ejects material (gases, liquids, pellets), causing the engine, and whatever is fastened to it, to move in the opposite direction. It develops very little thrust but more than enough to move a ship that is weightless.

Pellets of lunar rock will eventually be the material ejected by these engines. However, until a Moon base is able to supply these pellets, the ejected material will come from shuttle tanks. At the station in low-Earth orbit, tanks will be ground up and pulverized to provide material for the pellets.

Lunar Station

The mass-drive engine will push refitted tanks to lunar orbit. The tanks will be designed to lie on flat areas of the Moon's surface. The interiors will be modified to make living and recreation areas, as well as workshops. Each tank will have its own life-support equipment—food supplies, air, water, light, and temperature regulators. Once the

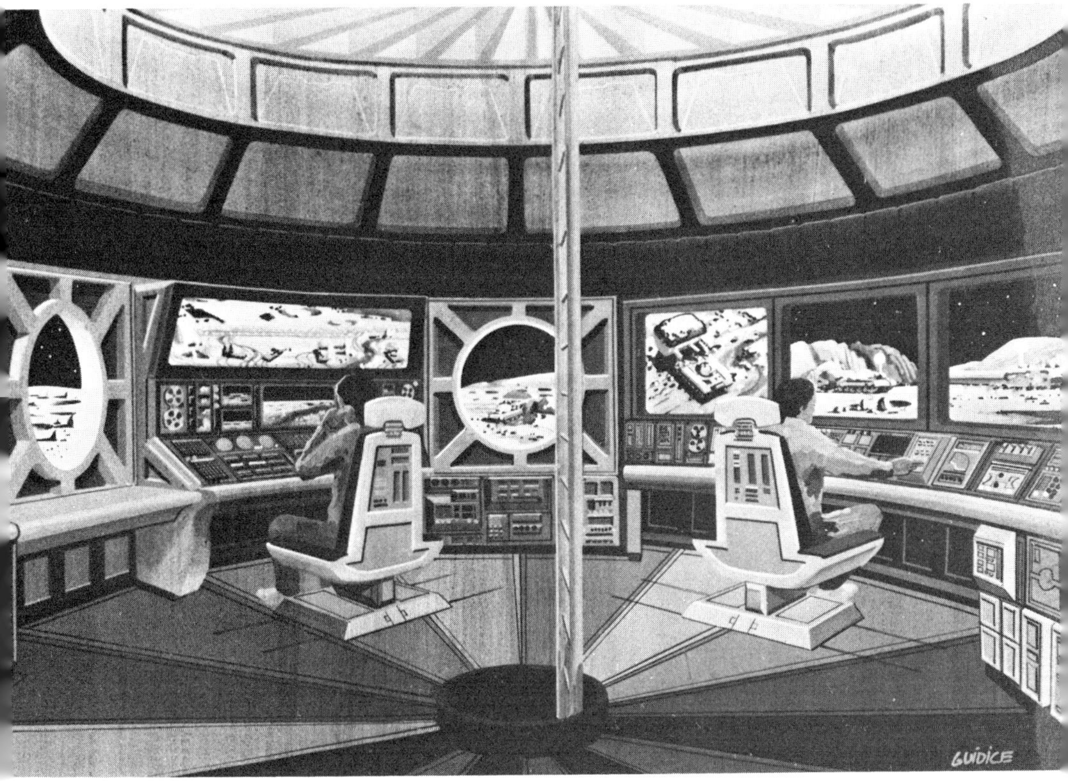

A control tower for lunar operations.

tanks and other Moon-base supplies are in orbit around the Moon, the mass-driver engine will detach and return to the space station.

Conventional rockets that burn chemical fuel will also be delivered to lunar orbit. They will go back and forth between the lunar surface and lunar orbit. Cables will connect the rockets to the tanks and to other payloads. The rockets will fire, taking the payload out of lunar orbit and putting it into a path that would crash it into the surface. However, the rocket will turn so that its exhaust is toward the Moon.

When it fires, the rocket will slow the fall toward the Moon. The payload will be soft-landed.

Two of the tanks will be used for rocket-fuel storage on the Moon. Once refueled, the rockets will return to lunar orbit, hook up to another payload, and take it in to the lunar station.

Shortly after the first lunar habitat is operating, engineers will set up solar collectors. These will be panels of solar cells that will supply electric power to the station. The station will be located in a flat lunar plain, and it will be exposed to direct sunlight for about two weeks. In that time, the collectors will produce the maximum amount of electricity.

During the two-week-long lunar night, there will be no direct sunlight. However, operations at the station will not shut down completely because large mirrors in lunar orbit will direct sunlight to the solar collectors. The mirrors will be in sunlight continuously. Light from them will still be sufficient for the collectors to operate at about 10 percent of full power. This will supply enough energy to keep the mining operation going, to keep life-support equipment functioning, and to light up the area.

Lunar Mass-Driver

Once the lunar station is operating, a major task will be to set up the lunar mass-driver. It will be the basic machine that makes the entire space colony idea workable. It ejects lunar rocks, gravel, and dust into space; and silicon, aluminum, and oxygen for the colony will be removed from the ore later.

Testing out the mass-driver.

The lunar mass-driver operates in much the same way as the mass-driver reaction engine. As pellets are ejected, the engine moves in the opposite direction. The mass-driver also ejects material, but the driver itself is fastened to the lunar surface, so it cannot move. Instead the lunar ore that it ejects flies into space at high speeds. The material is then caught by a mass-catcher and transferred to a processor that removes the metal from the ore.

The lunar mass-driver is not a new idea. The principle behind it was used by the Japanese to build an experimental railroad in the early 1970's. At a speed of only 20 miles per hour, the cars were lifted above the tracks by powerful magnets. They were moved ahead by straight-line electric motors. An electric motor turns because of magnetic attraction and repulsion. The same is true for a straight-line, or linear, motor, the difference being only that the attraction and repulsion are linear instead of circular. Just as a surfboard rides the leading edge of a wave in the sea, so the electric train rides on the leading edge of a magnetic wave. The speed and height of the wave are adjusted continually to accelerate the train and keep it moving smoothly.

The lunar mass-driver works in the same way. Lunar ore is crushed and placed in fiberglass bags. These bags are then put into buckets. The buckets may be compared to the cars of the experimental train in Japan. As they are lifted and held above the track by a magnetic field, the buckets are accelerated along the length of the driver to very high speeds. Along the way the paths of the buckets are corrected so that they are traveling absolutely straight. At the end of the driver, the bags are released. Because of their high speed, the bags leave the Moon and travel into space in a long, curving path. They are caught by a mass-catcher located some 75 000 kilometers above the far side of the Moon.

The picture shows the lunar base after installation is fairly complete. The modified shuttle tanks have been covered with lunar soil. This gives protection from cosmic rays and solar particles and it also is good insulation from the intense heat of the Sun. During the lunar night the insulation prevents loss of heat so that the temperature inside the tank is kept fairly even. The mass-driver is seen at the center extending to the right.

A lunar colony in full operation—mining ore on the surface and shipping it into space.

Chemical fuel for the rockets that travel between the Moon's surface and lunar orbit is stored under a section of the solar collector. There it is shielded from the Sun so that temperature remains very low, approximately equal to that of the lunar night.

The tunnel that surrounds the mass-driver can be seen reaching to the lunar horizon. Toward the end of the driver track, just over the horizon, the payload—the bags of lunar soil—is released. The buckets are then slowed down and turned around to make the return to the accelerator shed, where they will be reloaded.

The Mining Process

Mining the Moon will be quite different from mining on Earth. There will be no need to dig underground shafts or to go deep below the surface. The lunar surface is covered with loose material. Mining will consist of scooping up this rock, much of it pulverized. The process will continue into the lunar night when operations will be lighted by sunlight reflected from the large mirrors in orbit around the Moon.

One small truck operated by remote control will be sufficient in the beginning. Two or three other vehicles, much like bulldozers, perhaps, will level off areas for additional solar collectors. They will dig trenches for future facilities and place soil on top of the habitat and construction tanks.

Rapidly spinning flywheels, which will continue to spin for hours, will produce the energy to power lunar vehicles. The cars will have caterpillar drives, similar to those on military tanks. The vehicles will be repowered (the speed of the flywheels increased) by an electric motor that will receive its power from the solar collector panels.

Maintenance and repair of the vehicles, life-support equipment, sections of the mass-driver, and other devices will be done in a pressurized shuttle tank. It will have a large air lock 3 meters across and an open area approximately 20 meters long.

Rockets from lunar orbit will land 5 kilometers from the base. The soil in the landing-pad area will be treated with a binder to reduce dust that is thrown up by the rocket exhaust.

The habitat tank will be both the residence for personnel and the communications and control center. It will house ten persons, who will remain at the station for six months. At regular intervals, several times a year, three or four of the crew will be rotated either to Earth or to some other station in space—it might be the low-Earth orbit station or the space manufacturing base, which we'll discuss later. The lunar habitat will contain a center for communications and control, a main TV and recreational room, the galley and dining area, twelve private rooms with storage areas, and a section for the life-support equipment. Very likely, the tank will be sunk into the lunar surface, perhaps into a 3-meter ditch dug out by one of the lunar vehicles.

A person at the lunar station will see a slowly changing scene of mirrors following the Sun during the day and following the space reflectors during the two-week lunar night. The payloads ejected from the mass-driver will catch the sunlight and, because they will be close together (four or five per second), the payloads will appear as a sparkling line of light, something like a stream of water in sunlight.

The Mass-Catcher

Two days after launching, the bags of lunar ore will be moving in a stream 75 000 kilometers above the far side of the Moon. A mass-catcher will intercept them. This is a large cone-shaped bag 1200 meters long and 10 meters across at the mouth. A screen of heavy cable covers the mouth, and when a bag of lunar ore strikes the cables, the bag breaks and the bits of ore scatter into the cone. The entire cone rotates around the long axis (a line from the center of the opening to the tip). This rotation causes the ore to pack along the side of the cone, just as water in a pail is pushed to the bottom when the pail is swung around.

When the catcher is filled, it moves out of position and

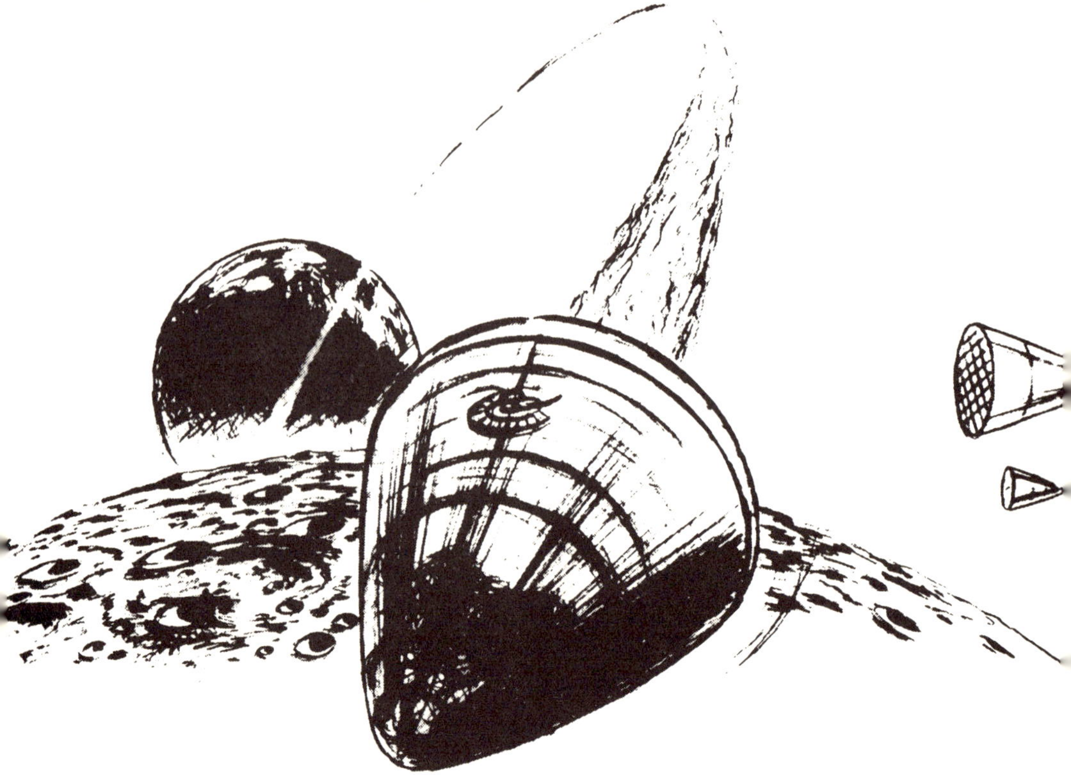

Packets of lunar ore are ejected into space. They are caught some 75 000 kilometers above the lunar surface.

makes a long, slow trip to the site of the space colony, some 300 000 kilometers from Earth. As it proceeds, another catcher moves into position to catch the bags of ore.

The catchers are moved by pellet launchers. The launchers work for the same reason that a rocket works—when hot exhaust gases are ejected, the rocket goes in the opposite direction. The pellet launchers will throw out pellets of lunar ore instead of gases. Therefore, the launcher itself, and the mass-catcher to which it is fastened, will move in the opposite direction.

A pellet-making machine aboard the catcher crushes

lunar ore and presses it into the pellets that are fed to the launcher. These are then ejected, pushing the catcher through space. Brief action of the launcher holds the catcher in position to obtain the lunar ore. During the flight to the colony site, the launcher operates continually. It exerts only a small force but this force is all that is needed to move a large mass through space.

3

The Construction Station

The materials needed for a space colony weigh hundreds of thousands of tons. Transporting everything from Earth would require thousands of shuttle launchings, which would use up much more fuel than Earth's resources could supply. Even if those materials—silicon, oxygen, aluminum, iron, and other metals—were obtained on the Moon and the products manufactured there, as has been suggested, and then sent into space, the cost would still be much too high. For one thing, the finished products would have to be lifted from the lunar surface, and chemical rockets would be needed to do this. Therefore, a large part of the chemicals would have to come from Earth, making them outrageously expensive.

The only reasonable procedure is to fabricate products in space, using as raw materials the ores found on the lunar surface and throwing them into space with a mass-driver such as the one discussed earlier.

Station in low-Earth orbit. The two large modules in the middle of the picture, each about the size of a large mobile home, serve as living quarters for a crew of eight. The smaller module (partially covered with thermal insulation) serves as a storeroom for consumable items such as food, water and liquid rocket fuel. A space shuttle is just arriving with supplies.

The lunar ore is thrown some 75 000 kilometers beyond the far side of the Moon, where it is collected in the mass-catcher. From there, the ore is carried to a colony, as mentioned earlier, or to a separate construction station. The station itself will be assembled in space, using materials brought from Earth. This will be done in low-Earth orbit,

The construction base will include a factory for processing lunar ore. Workers will live in the small cylinders at the ends of the arms. The arms and the cylinders rotate to provide "gravity." The large sphere does not rotate.

probably some 250 kilometers above the surface. Once the station has been assembled, small chemical rockets (or perhaps a mass-driver engine) will push the station out some 300 000 kilometers and place it in final orbit. At that location a minimum amount of energy will be needed to transport lunar ore to it from the site of the mass-catcher.

The station's work area will probably be a sphere about 100 meters across. A large part of it will be taken up by the equipment used for removing silicon, oxygen, aluminum, iron, and titanium from lunar ore. A hollow cylinder some 50 meters long will extend from the sphere. Hollow arms 500 meters long will extend outward from this cylinder, much like the spokes of a wheel. The crew will live in small cylinders attached to these "spokes," which will rotate two to three times per minute to produce an artificial gravity.

Since the large sphere, the work area, will not rotate, there will be zero gravity in that section. When people report to the work area, they will go through the long hollow arms to the central cylinder. There they will dress in space suits and then move into the large ball through an air lock.

Zero gravity, or weightlessness, in the work area will enable a person to move large masses of material easily. Zero gravity will make it possible to produce metals that are free from impurities. No container will be needed to hold these metals; their own mass will hold them together.

Energy for the construction station will come from the Sun. Collectors located a short distance from the station will harness solar energy and convert it into electricity. As we will see in Chapter 7, constructing these solar collectors will be a major purpose of early space manufacturing.

Large amounts of energy are needed to produce metals from ores. For example, the complex steps necessary to obtain aluminum include melting the ore and quenching the hot ore with water. Then the ore is mixed with sulfuric acid, baked at high temperature, and combined with chlorine. In the final stage an electric current is passed through the mixture to separate the metal from the ore. The process is involved and in space it would be expensive, costing about

$10 a pound. On Earth a pound of aluminum costs about $1. However, if this Earth-made aluminum were sent to the station from Earth, the cost of transportation would push the price up to about $40 a pound.

Materials needed to process the metals will come from Earth. Efficient methods will reduce waste, so many of the materials will be recycled. Once the station is operating, it will be able to sustain itself, for the most part. The aluminum obtained will be shaped into beams and sheets and whatever other forms are needed to build the space colony.

Constructing the Colony

Lunar-ore processing will be done inside the construction station, but construction of the colony will take place outside the station. This means that the crew will have to wear space suits, which are clumsy and awkward. In most cases, the workers will have to be tethered to the station or to sections of the colony as they take shape. To make them more comfortable and to permit them to work for longer time periods, some of them will probably operate remote-control assemblers.

One worker stands inside a closed capsule. Jets attached to it can move the capsule in any direction. Once it is in position, the operator, by moving controls inside the capsule, will move jointed arms with pincers that can grasp metal beams and girders and bring them together. Explosive charges are ignited to weld the beams together or to weld sheets to the beams. Subassemblies are built and joined together, and so the colony takes shape.

Large assemblies can be put together in space. Here panels of a colony are being fitted in place. The small vehicles are called ANTS for Assembly Non-Tethered Ships

The torus itself, the "tire" of the colony, is built in sections. After completion of the outer shell, the ends are closed, making a sealed cylinder which is then pressurized, that is, filled with air so that workers can continue their work inside, in a shirt-sleeve environment—without space suits.

As the torus sections are completed, they are joined together. Meanwhile, other workers are assembling the central hub of the colony, the docking facility, and the long hollow spokes of the "wheel." Sections for living and farming are covered with plates of lunar slag, the material left after the usable products have been removed from the lunar ore. The plates make a shield to protect against cosmic particles. (We'll talk more about these particles in Chapter 8.)

After years of activity, including hundreds of shuttle flights, the mining of millions of tons of lunar ore and the processing of this ore at the construction station, Colony Two will become a reality. Thousands of colonists such as Jenny and Tom, who wrote the letter in Chapter 1, will live and work there. And they will continue to communicate with their Earth-based families.

January 2070
Vega Drive
Colony Two

Dear Peggy and Arthur,

We enjoyed talking to you on the videophone. Both of you looked well tanned, so you must be spending some time in the sun.

As we mentioned, most of the people now at the Colony intend to spend their lives here. In the past year or so, several families have returned to Earth. For one reason or another, they wanted to go back. Many of them, it seems to us, returned because they were homesick for their families. Others could not find a place for themselves once the job they were sent here for was finished.

We are now both working part-time on Colony Three, in addition to our jobs on the new power satellites that are being built for a group of Earth-based electric companies. These improved collectors will be much more efficient than the old ones, and I understand they will pay for themselves after only six or seven years of operation. If all goes well—that is, if there is no breakdown at the construction station or at the lunar mining station—we should finish the first of this new generation of power satellites in three years.

But the really exciting topic here is Colony Three. The first of a new generation of colonies, it has been designed for sixty thousand people. Instead of being wheel-shaped, it will be spherical—at least the habitat area will be. Agricultural regions will be tirelike sections outside the sphere. Just about everyone here is working on some part of Colony Three. Most of the design work has been completed, and subassembly of sections has started, although I suspect we won't go all out with it until the first new power satellite has been completed.

Another big piece of news—we are now part of the government—Jenny was elected by our section to serve on the Council. She's one of nine members, including the chairperson. You may recall that the Colony was developed in a joint venture by the U.S. government and private industry.

Private industry sure stimulates activity here. Gradually, as the Colony manufactures more and more products, the people are "paying off" the different companies. Part of Jenny's job in the Council is to keep track of who owns what, and to record payments as they are made. (We now own about 90 percent of our living quarters, and should pay off the rest in a couple of years.) Everyone here is prosperous; there are jobs for everyone. A really important thing is that people are here because this is where they want to be and they enjoy doing their jobs.

Jenny and I were reminiscing the other night about the trips we used to take by car to the National Parks. There's nothing like that here. However, friends of ours (the Japanese couple we met on the trip out) have vacationed on the Moon. They rented a small vehicle that they "flew" to low lunar orbit. There they transferred to a lunar lander, which took only a few minutes to set them down on the Moon's surface. They spent three days there, exploring the valleys of the Moon and visiting the different sections of the mining operation. Sounded like quite an interesting trip, one that Jenny and I would like to take for a holiday. Food was pretty limited, though, because the lunar farms aren't as large as ours, and there were only a few basic items available—very few fruits and berries, and no fish at all.

One evening a week we both take courses in computer programming, and I'm taking a refresher in solid-state troubleshooting. Jenny teaches music, of course, and then there's that international cooking course we're both taking. But we manage to stay slim, in spite of all the good dishes we come up with.

Drop us a line when you get a chance. It was good to see you and talk with you on the videophone and we always enjoy reading your letters.

Love
Jenny and Tom

The letter gives a few hints about the work and ways of living in Colony Two. We'll take a closer look at some of them.

7

Work Aboard Colony Two

In space, sunlight is intense. The Sun shines steadily all the time; there is neither an atmosphere to filter it nor clouds to block it. Thus space is perfect for capturing solar energy for heat or electricity. The entire space colony idea is based on the easy accessibility of sunlight. Moon mining will be powered by the Sun as will the mass-drivers on the Moon and space vehicles of various kinds. All the energy for space manufacturing, for farming, and for heating and cooling entire colonies will be solar.

Solar-Power Satellites

An early space manufacturing and construction project will be the building of solar satellites to capture energy for use on Earth. In fact, a major source of money to support the development of space manufacturing will come from the selling of solar-generated electricity to Earth-based homes and industries.

The remaining years of the twentieth century and the beginning of the twenty-first century will be a time of transition from fossil energy (gas, coal, and oil) to various kinds of renewable energy. Among these will be wind power, nuclear fusion (we hope), geothermal energy, ocean thermal electric energy, and, of course, solar energy. Many obstacles will have to be overcome before solar energy can be developed, but there are three that cannot be surmounted—the fact that there is night (solar energy is turned off), the existence of clouds, which often dim the Sun and so reduce sharply the energy that an area receives, and the absence of intense year-round sunlight in those parts of the world where the energy need is greatest.

Because of these problems, the most efficient collectors of solar energy will have to be located where sunlight falls on them twenty-four hours a day, where there are no clouds, and where a distance of a few hundred miles farther north or south does not matter—in short, in outer space.

Many of the engineering details have already been worked out, and the first test satellite is being planned for the early 1990's. It will consist of a large panel of solar cells. These cells, similar to the ones now operating in space probes and communication satellites, will convert sunlight into electricity. The electricity, in turn, will be changed to microwaves, much like the waves in a microwave oven, but

A solar-cell power satellite may look like this huge panel some 20 kilometers long and 6 across. Antennas at either end of the panel transmit the power to Earth by microwave.

more powerful. A special antenna on the satellite will beam the radio waves toward a receiving antenna on Earth. There, at the receiving station, the waves will be converted to a current of electricity and carried by wires to cities and towns.

The satellite will orbit some 36 000 kilometers above Earth, and it will have a revolution period of twenty-four hours, the same as Earth's period of rotation. This means the satellite will always remain above the same Earth location, in line with the receiving antenna. Night and day, year in and year out, the beam of energy will be sent to Earth.

By the time this first power satellite is built, hopefully the cost of solar cells will have come down. In the early 1980's solar cells cost several thousand dollars per square meter, which makes them much too expensive to be used in the panels of a power satellite that would extend over thousands of square meters.

Even if no way is found to reduce the cost, another method of generating solar electricity is available. Power satellites can be made of panels of mirrors rather than solar cells. The mirrors focus sunlight onto boilers that produce hot gases, and these gases turn turbine generators. The electricity produced is converted to microwaves, which are beamed to Earth and distributed in the same manner.

Not everyone agrees that these methods of generating electricity are feasible. Some engineers say that the cost will be so high that even though the electricity is sold, it will take ages for the investment to show a profit.

Other groups have also raised objections against power satellites. If the panels are as large as planned, 4 or 5 kilometers on a side, the satellite will be a bright object, perhaps as bright as the full Moon. Astronomers argue that under those conditions their large telescopes would not be very useful, since they operate best when the sky is as dark as possible.

Radio astronomers, on the other hand, fear that spillovers of the microbeam from the satellite might occur, which would seriously interfere with the reception of weak radio waves from deep space. These waves contain very little energy, often no more than the energy that would be received on Earth from a match flaming on the surface of Mars. Even the slightest interference of such a weak signal cannot be overcome.

Many biologists are also concerned. They fear that the microbeam might not be focused properly and, as a result, might fall and harm people, animals, and plants. And then there is always the possibility that the microbeam might change the ozone layer of the atmosphere. Ozone is a form of oxygen that has the ability to filter ultraviolet radiation. It protects Earth from receiving large amounts of these rays, which are hazardous to people and animals, as well as to many plants.

All these arguments against power satellites must be examined and weighed carefully. They may prove to be groundless, or at least less alarming than has been feared. Perhaps ways may be found to eliminate the dangers. Let us hope so, for it seems that solar-power satellites might be the solution to many of the world's energy problems. Certainly these satellites will be essential for furnishing the energy needed to develop space structures.

Eventually colonists may build huge solar-thermal-electric generators like this. Solar energy is converted to heat which, in turn, drives turbines. The shuttle shown upside down at upper right gives some idea of the size of such a structure.

Satellite Repair

Once solar-power satellites are operating, they will require maintenance. Particles from the Sun may wear away the solar cells. There may be collisions with meteoroids—small bits of metal and stone that abound in space. And there will be breakdowns that result from less-than-perfect construction. Repair crews will journey from the space colony to the satellites.

Space colonists may use small vehicles to move in close to satellites of various kinds to make repairs. Notice the multiple wrench the astronaut is carrying.

They will move through space on specialized small vehicles designed to carry crews of three or four workers. The ships will carry life-support equipment, so travelers will not have to wear space suits. The tugs, as they may be called, will take off from the docking hub. Little power will be needed to launch them under zero gravity; there will be no need to climb out of a "gravity hole," as discussed in Chapter 2. Similarly, little power will be needed to move the ship close to the power satellite.

Tugs will also be used for repairing other kinds of satellites, another major task of the colonists. Since the late 1960's and early 1970's, hundreds of satellites have been put into orbit—satellites for observing weather, for carrying telephone and television messages, for surveying the Earth, for military surveillance.

These satellites are powered either by solar cells or by small nuclear-electric generators, and although the equipment is carefully made, nothing works forever. When a satellite fails to function properly, it will be an easy matter for a space tug to intercept it. If repairs are minor, a worker will get into a space suit, leave the tug, and make the corrections. Should the satellite need more attention, it might be towed back to the colony, where major problems would be corrected.

Industries and governments that use the satellites will pay the costs of these repairs, another source of income for a colony. And the repair costs will be much lower than the cost of replacing the satellite and launching the replacement into orbit.

Growing Crystals

Under zero gravity and high vacuum, it is possible to grow perfect crystals because material does not settle, as mentioned in Chapter 2. Another advantage is that there is no pollution. Crystals grown in space have an even structure; they are pure. Such crystals are needed to control electric circuits in delicate equipment. Many experts believe also that it will be possible to grow strips of silicon crystals—the kind needed for solar cells. If this is so, then the cost of producing large solar converters will drop from thousands of dollars for a square meter to only a few dollars, making possible the solar-power satellites we talked about. When such crystals are available in quantity and solar-power satellites have become a reality, it should be possible to furnish electricity to Earth at low cost—perhaps for less than one cent per kilowatt hour, a fraction of what the price has been since the energy crisis began.

Improved crystals will be a valuable product of a space colony, but certainly not profitable enough to pay the costs of building a colony. However, the electricity derived from power satellites using silicon crystals could return billions of dollars. Even more important, this electricity will free the world from dependence on fossil fuels—and conserve for other uses the valuable chemicals found in coal, gas, and oil.

Such a move will eliminate much pollution. Since electricity is a much cleaner source of energy, air and water on Earth will also be cleaner. The outlook is exciting.

Optical Telescope

Of equal interest and excitement is the possibility of building a super telescope. On Earth, gravity limits the size of an optical telescope. For one thing, the telescope gets too heavy, since weight is simply a measurement of the gravity exerted on a mass of material. The great weight (force of gravity) causes the glass to sag. This means that the curves of the lenses or mirrors cannot be made perfect. As a consequence, the lenses cannot focus sharply, and thus the use of the telescope is limited.

In space it is possible to make perfect lenses and mirrors. The glass will be flawless and of uniform quality throughout. It will still be difficult to mold large lenses, however, and so the space telescope will probably be made of thousands of mirrors rather than lenses. Each mirror will be about a meter across and arranged to cover an extended region, perhaps a kilometer on a side. The array of small mirrors will function as though there were one single mirror of that size. Light from each mirror will be brought to a single point and focused by a series of perfect lenses.

A space telescope of such dimensions might be able to detect planets that are moving around distant stars. If there are such planets, and provided they are large enough, the telescope might be able to "see" them even if they should be a hundred light-years away. (A light-year is 10 trillion kilometers—the distance light travels in a year.) From Earth planets only five or ten light-years away would be much too dim to be visible. Presently, many astronomers suspect that planets associated with distant stars may exist, but there is no way of detecting them.

Radio Telescope

In the 1960's and 1970's, radio telescopes searched space for signs of intelligent life beyond Earth. They were tuned to receive the kind of signals that a civilization out among the stars might be broadcasting.

At first the telescopes were low power, and they could not be focused sharply. Over the years telescopes were improved. They could detect very weak radio waves, and they could focus accurately enough to determine exactly the location of the source of the waves, should any be detected.

Waves from many different sources were found. All of them were produced naturally—in a star, for example, on the surface of a planet, or in space itself. No radio wave that might have been produced by radio equipment—that is, by intelligent creatures—has ever been detected.

Many people do not accept this as proof that there are no creatures out there. The fault, they say, is in our equipment. We need more sensitive telescopes. When we have them, and when we tune them properly and point them in the right direction, then we'll pick up radio signals from another world—so they believe. There are a lot of stars, at least a hundred billion in our own galaxy; and there are billions of galaxies. Surely, among this stupendous number of stars there must be hundreds or millions that have planets. And among that great number of planets there must be at least thousands that support life of some kind.

Belief in the existence of intelligent creatures beyond the Earth is so strong that many people feel a major task of the space colonists will be to continue the search. It could be that the colonists will pick up a radio signal, proof positive that radio engineers live on a far-off world. Radio telescopes built in a space colony would have a much greater chance of doing this than the telescopes we can build on Earth.

Since weight is not a factor in space, a radio telescope can be made very large. The space-colony telescope may be a single large dish antenna, perhaps 5 kilometers across. It would be able to receive waves over the entire surface and relay them to a single receiver.

A major problem with radio telescopes is interference. Radio and TV stations fill space with radio waves. The radio telescope receiver must be able to blot out all those waves and pick up only the ones from outer space. A telescope mounted close to the space colony could do this. Interference would be eliminated by placing a disk-shaped metal baffle between Earth and the telescope. Radio waves could not go through the baffle, and so the only waves reaching the telescope would be those from outside the Earth. Signals might come from distant stars, or perhaps from creatures living on far-off Planet X.

The telescope need not have much strength. It could be little more than a framework covered by a thin film of aluminum. The structure would be much less complex than a solar-powered satellite. Because of its space location, the telescope could survey any part of the universe at any time. Also, it could lock on to a particular star or distant planet and keep pointing at it for days, weeks, or months if necessary.

Magnets

Magnets are metals in which the molecules are in a uniform arrangement. In space such magnets could be made more perfectly, for there is no gravitational force exerted on the molecules. Because of their freedom from a gravitational field, the molecules can move without restraint and line up

A huge radio telescope shielded from Earth will enable astronomers to pick up very weak radio waves. The space shuttle, and its shadow, show how large the receiver might be.

without exception. Therefore, magnets made in space are very strong, and the magnetism will last virtually forever.

Magnets are used extensively in all sorts of electronic equipment to control the flow of electricity, in spectrographs to separate material by mass, and in electronic motors of all kinds. Superior magnets produce superior equipment. Super magnets will be important products of space colonies.

8

Hazards in Space

March 2070
Vega Drive
Colony Two

Dear Peggy and Arthur,

This letter is to give you more details than we could on the videophone of our recent disaster.

As you know, we are in Earth orbit, which means we're more or less controlled by Earth's gravitation, just as the Moon is. So, while Earth goes around the Sun, we're carried along with it. We knew from our detecting equipment that we were going to pass through a meteor-swarm, but the safety engineers didn't think there would be any massive particles. They expected them to be the size of grains of sand, mostly, with perhaps occasionally a somewhat larger object, certainly nothing as large as the baseball-size masses that crashed into the Colony. A few hours before they hit we saw them, but it was too late to do little more than put the repair crews on standby.

Well, as you know, we were bombarded. Fortunately the slag layer around the colony protected us from most of the hits, but there were six that broke through almost at the same moment. It was a freak situation that will probably never occur again; let's hope not.

Atmosphere escaped rapidly through the breaks, so it was essential for the crews to repair them quickly. And they did, for the most part. Metal plates were put over the holes and held in place with spot welds.

Really quite easy: the hardest part was getting to the breaks, all of which were high above the living level. Tugs similar to those used outside the Colony were used. Jets moved them into position and held them in place during the repairs.

However, that wasn't the only problem. One of the meteoroids (probably the largest one, or one that came in at just the right angle) made a direct hit on the mechanism that controls the solar mirrors. These move so that the amount of sunshine inside each section of the Colony can be regulated. The mirrors were stuck in a position that caused the full intensity of the Sun to fall on vegetable crops that were about to be harvested. The agriculture experts warned frantically that the crops would be burned badly unless the condition was corrected right away.

Ordinarily, this is no particular problem—a repair team goes out in a tug or on tethers and does the job. That's what was done and all went well until one woman worker got snarled in the jagged edges made by the collision. Her suit was ripped badly which is the worst disaster that can happen. Pressure on her dropped immediately to zero, and of course it was all over in a moment. No one could do anything for her. It's the first tragedy of that kind we've had here. The entire Colony is saddened, but we all realize there are hazards wherever one lives, perhaps a bit more here in Colony Two than elsewhere.

Fortunately the repairs were soon made at all the collision areas. We were back in operation within ninety minutes, and the crops escaped completely. It's reassuring to know that we can meet a major calamity head-on like that.

Both of us have recovered from the scare and the shock—even though we didn't know the woman who was killed, most of us felt as though we had lost a member of the family.

Next time, hopefully, we'll be writing about happier events. All is well here now. Work moves steadily on the construction of Colony Three.

Love,
Jenny and Tom

It is true that there are hazards and dangers wherever one lives. But it is also true that there are additional and unusual hazards to face in a space colony.

Meteoroids

A meteoroid collision such as the one described in the letter would be very rare. There might be an occasional crash, but a series of hits occurring close together would be exceptional. Man-made satellites have been flying around the Earth for years. Some of them have had counters aboard to measure collisions with meteoroids. Impacts are so unusual that some of the satellites measure zero even after several years of exposure.

Space teems with meteoroids. For the most part, these are small bits of iron and stone between the planets. The particles are so small that a better name for them is micrometeoroids. Most meteoroids are like bits of dust; they have little more substance than a tiny piece of a cigarette ash. Larger meteoroids are much rarer. Even a meteoroid weighing one gram (one thirtieth of an ounce) is unusual. Most of them are much smaller than that, down to a billionth of a gram. However, every now and then a large meteoroid appears, the size of a marble, let us say, or a Ping-Pong ball. The space colony must be prepared for collisions with them and with even larger ones.

The windows in a colony will be the parts most easily damaged. To reduce hazards, they will be made of small panels, not much larger than the window in the door of a car. Each window will be set in a metal framework that will provide strength, so that the glass itself need not support any weight. If one window is broken, there will be no decrease in the strength of the structure.

Collisions with meteoroids large enough to break a window should occur no more often than once every thousand years or so. If such a collision does happen, there will be a sudden loss of pressure and air will escape. With it, there will also be a loss of water vapor. Just outside the colony, a white cloud will appear as the water vapor freezes into ice crystals.

As soon as a window is broken, it will set off alarms instantly, and repair crews will hurry to the location at once. They will ride in a service car along the monorail used for transport until they reach the proper cross-structure, where the car will detach and then move by jets to the broken window. Once there, the crew will routinely repair the damage by setting a new window into the metal framework.

Since most such repairs can be made from inside the colony, an incident will cause no panic. Indeed, most of the colonists will not even be aware of the collision, for there will be no serious loss of air, and the repair can easily be made within an hour or so.

Even though larger meteoroids are extremely rare, it is still possible that one might hit a space colony. One as large as a car, for example, would cause major damage, but not a disaster. People in that section of the colony would be moved out quickly and the section closed off. Inside repairs would be made in the same way as when a window is broken. At the same time, repair crews would work on the outside of the colony. Space-suited workers would be tethered to the colony as they repaired panels by welding them into place, and gradually the structure would be rebuilt. The colony will be designed to make the various segments independent, so that even though one of the six sections may be damaged and not usable, the other five sections will continue to function.

Radiation

Every day of our lives each of us is exposed to radiation—energy given off by nuclei of atoms. The radiation comes from small amounts of radioactive materials in our bodies—obtained from food, air, and perhaps water. It may also be contained in the bricks and stones in our houses, or in the rocks and soil in the neighborhood. In some parts of the world, this amounts to quite a lot of radiation. Fortunately, most of the radiation we receive has little or no effect on us.

In a space colony, there will be no rocks and soil from Earth, so there will be no radiation from those sources. (There is very little radiation from lunar rocks.) But cosmic-ray particles are present in full strength. Cosmic rays are bits and pieces of the cores of atoms. They are filtered by our atmosphere, and so are low power when they reach Earth—we are not affected by them. But in space, cosmic-ray particles are not filtered. They can penetrate a space suit, a metal covering, and even stony material. Exposure to these particles over a long period of time could be harmful.

In addition to those particles that make up the background cosmic radiation, occasionally there are more powerful particles. These are called heavy particles, and they can destroy cells in various parts of the body. Men who have spent considerable time in space have been exposed to them, and no doubt some brain cells and other cells in the body have been destroyed by them. But no long-term ill effects have been noticed in any of our astronauts. Nevertheless, a space colony will have to be protected against the particles.

It will also have to guard against particles that are ejected from the Sun. Every once in a while a small section of the Sun ejects high-energy particles into space. They travel at high speeds, and someone struck by them would be seriously injured. Very likely, a person would not survive direct exposure.

An important task in a space colony will be that of solar monitoring. Instruments aimed at the Sun will be sensitive to slight changes in the Sun. As soon as something unusual is detected, a solar flare, for example, the entire colony will be notified. People will move out of the hub and spokes (regions that are not shielded) and into the torus. Two-thirds of the torus will be covered with a "stone" wall made out of slag. This wall will not repel particles, but it will remove some of the energy from them and so make them less harmful.

The glass-window part of the torus will be covered with aluminum V-shaped strips. These will also remove energy from cosmic particles. With adequate shielding, the amount of radiation in the space colony will be reduced to levels low enough to be safe, even over an entire lifetime. None of the colonists—not even repair crews—will spend much time outside the structure, because continued exposure to radiation in outer space, even at low levels, might be harmful to humans. It is very likely that robots will be used where working conditions are hazardous.

Zero Gravity

The human body has developed under conditions of gravity. The heart must pump blood upward, against gravity, as well as in other directions; body fluids tend to move downward and organs of the body are also pulled downward because of gravity. Therefore, a person has to get used to zero gravity. Most people become "space sick" when they first experience it, but they generally recover quickly. Others may take two or three days before they feel better. Some people never get used to zero gravity.

There will be "gravity" in the torus of the space colony. But the force will drop rapidly as a person moves toward the hub. Outside the colony a person will be completely weightless. Most of the colonists will spend the larger part of their lives in the torus area. However, there will be occasions in everyone's life for moving into the hub region.

People will also want to take vacations away from the colony. They might take a trip to the Moon base or the construction station. Some might even visit Earth. Or a family might rent a space-camper to journey to a neighbor colony, one in a different Earth-orbit.

People who grow up in the colony will probably adjust easily to zero gravity. Older people, who have spent part of their lives on Earth, may become nauseous until they adjust to weightlessness. A person exposed to zero gravity for only a short time will not feel ill effects other than nausea. Workmen who have to spend longer periods of time in zero gravity will have to be checked closely.

Under gravity the blood tends to "pool" in the legs—

pulled down by gravity. Without gravity, there is no pooling. The body reacts as though there were a sudden increase in body fluids. To adjust, it throws off liquids. Long exposure to zero gravity tends to decrease the amount of blood. Also, calcium and phosphorous are lost in one's urine.

Another problem in zero gravity is the loss of muscle tone. Our muscles must "work" in order to be healthy. We know this, because we feel lazy if we don't exercise—our muscles lose tone. In zero gravity the muscles work very little because it is easy to move about, and no effort is needed to stand or sit erect. There is no walking in space; one gets about by "floating" or by moving from strap to strap—from handhold to handhold.

Workers will probably be cycled—they will spend only a few days, or weeks perhaps, in zero gravity. Then they will be transferred to a work area such as a recycling plant or another factory in the torus, where they will be subjected to gravity and their muscles will have to go to work.

A few Americans and Russians have been in space for several months. In all cases, their bodies adjusted to the weightless condition. Loss of body fluids stopped, and no harm from cosmic rays was apparent. But exposure to space conditions for longer periods, for years and lifetimes, may be harmful to people, although most scientists believe otherwise. From the knowledge we now have of the way people adjust to space, scientists think that the body will do as well in outer space as on Earth, especially when people are born there and spend their entire lives in a colony.

9

Century 21 and Beyond

The main purpose of early space colonies will be to support Earth. Technicians and engineers will build and service solar-power satellites, grow perfect crystals for all kinds of electronic devices, perhaps produce serums for the treatment of disease, fabricate special alloys, and no doubt research and develop devices no one has yet anticipated. Eventually, however, colonies will exist because people will want to spend their lives there.

The pleasant "weather," opportunities to do research under space conditions, to explore for life in the universe, to learn ways of using zero gravity and a high vacuum, to practice a profession—medicine, law, education—and to set up new business ventures in stimulating surroundings will have wide appeal. Eventually there may be colonies that hold a million people or more. But before such super colonies are built, there will be "second-generation" col-

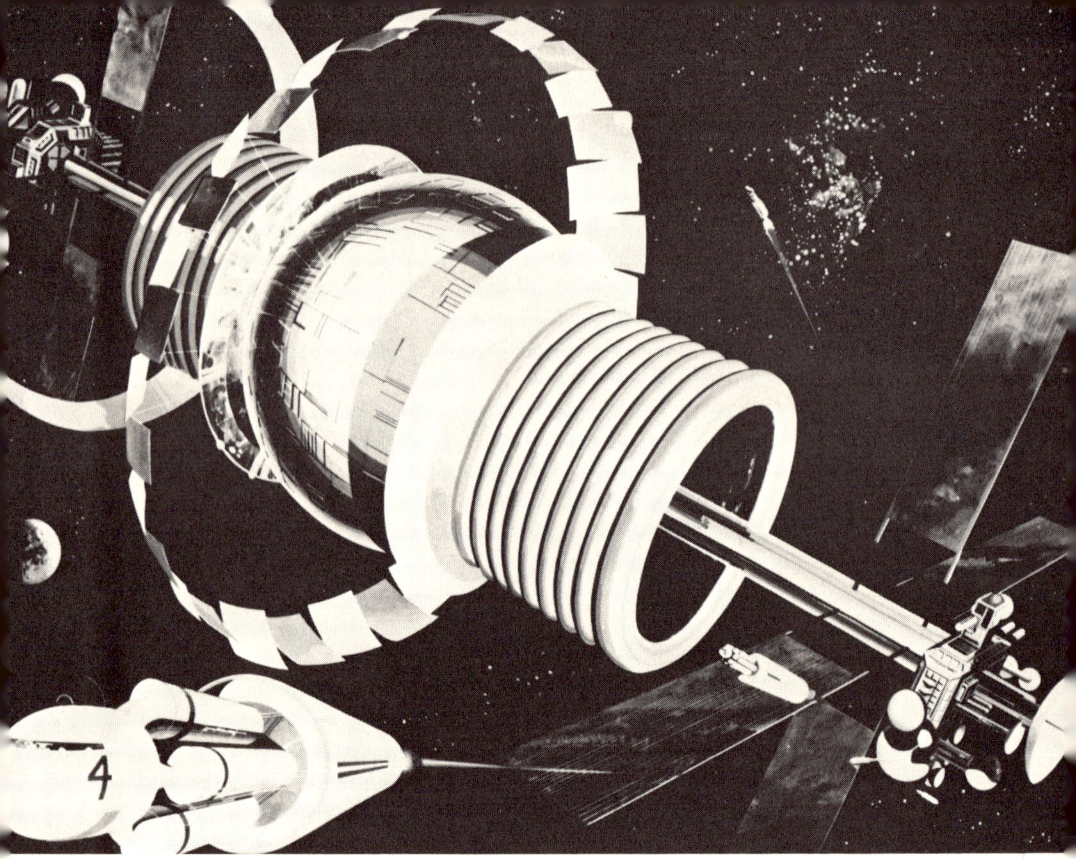

The residential area of Colony Three is the central sphere. Farming regions are in the "tires." Mirrors reflect sunlight into the habitat and farms. The large flat panels radiate away extra heat into space, and panels of solar cells provide electricity. Factories and docks for spaceships are at either end of the long central tube.

onies. Very likely these will be spherical, and they may hold a hundred thousand people, as has been suggested by many engineers and scientists.

Colony Three

Colony Three, mentioned briefly in the letters sent from Colony Two, is a sphere some 500 meters (over a quarter of a mile) in diameter. The inner surface of the sphere contains apartments, stores, public buildings, and parks for many thousands of people. The sphere spins to provide artificial gravity, which is strongest along the equator region. As one moves away from the equator, gravitation decreases; thus movement is less strenuous. Perhaps a stream flows around the equator. It would certainly add to the scenery, and fish could be raised in it.

Large hollow tubes are fastened to the top and bottom of the sphere. Through these, colonists can reach the farm areas, a series of tirelike formations in which grains and vegetables are grown and livestock is raised. The tubes receive sunlight for up to twenty hours a day, making it possible to grow crops rapidly and for plants to be very productive. Factories that require intense heat or zero gravity or that produce wastes are located at the far end of one of the tubes, about a kilometer away from the residential area.

The end of the other tube contains docking areas for space vehicles, a hospital for patients who benefit by being in zero gravity, and factories for manufacturing small items such as microchips for computers, precision lenses, and small super magnets. Transportation through the tubes is by monorail cars driven by small compressed air jets; they use no fuel and give off no waste products. Sunlight is controlled by movable mirrors. The residential section has a regular day-night cycle, whereas the factory region is in full-intensity sunlight and the farming areas have a prolonged day with a very short night (a brief resting period for the plants). Electricity is generated by "dishes" of solar cells arranged in "collars" around the top and bottom of the sphere.

As in all space installations, heat builds up, so it has to be disposed of. Extra heat from the interior is conducted to large flat metal vanes, which radiate the heat into space. As in earlier colonies, the inside of the sphere is air-conditioned with the temperature kept at a constant 20– 22 degrees Celsius and a humidity level of about 40– 45 percent.

Colony Four

In the twenty-first century there may be space colonies much larger than any we have discussed—maybe large enough to support a million people or more.

The main part of Colony Four is a cylinder about 6 kilometers in diameter and 30 kilometers long, as long as Manhattan Island. The entire colony rotates along the long axis to provide an artificial gravity by pushing everything toward the outer wall. Colonists would live in three strips running the length of the cylinder, with alternating strips covered with "windows" separating them.

Large, movable mirrors outside the cylinder reflect sunlight into the colony. By moving the mirrors in a certain way, the Sun appears to rise, move across the sky, and then set to provide a day-night cycle. The timing of this varies, so that the living areas do not all follow the same cycle—some areas have day while others experience night. At the ends of the cylinders are other large curved mirrors which collect sunlight and concentrate it on electric generators. Since the production of electricity is uninterrupted, there is an ample supply of energy for all the colony's requirements.

Food for the colony is grown in cylinders. About a

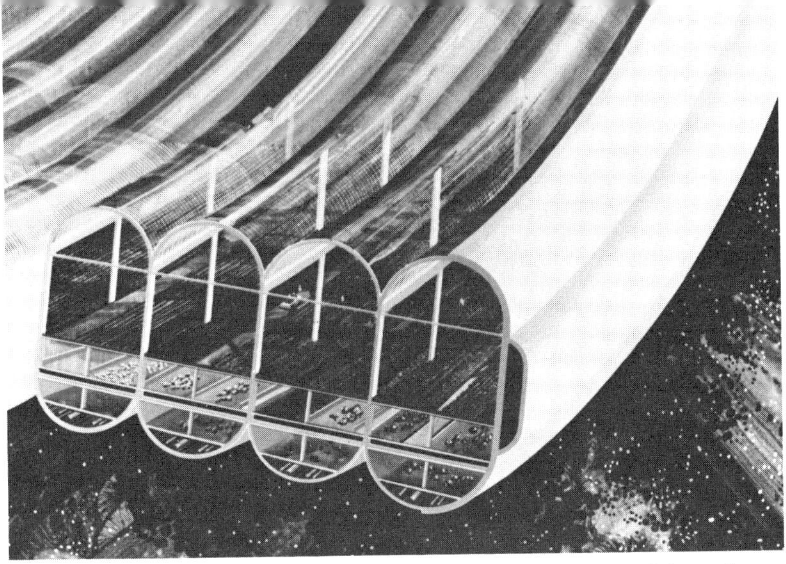

A series of farming sections, all located inside the "tires" of the colony.

Inside the sphere. Gravity is strongest along the equator. As one moves toward the center, gravity lessens, and one could fly easily. Sunlight enters as shown by the large fuzzy ring. The central tube connects to other sections of the colony.

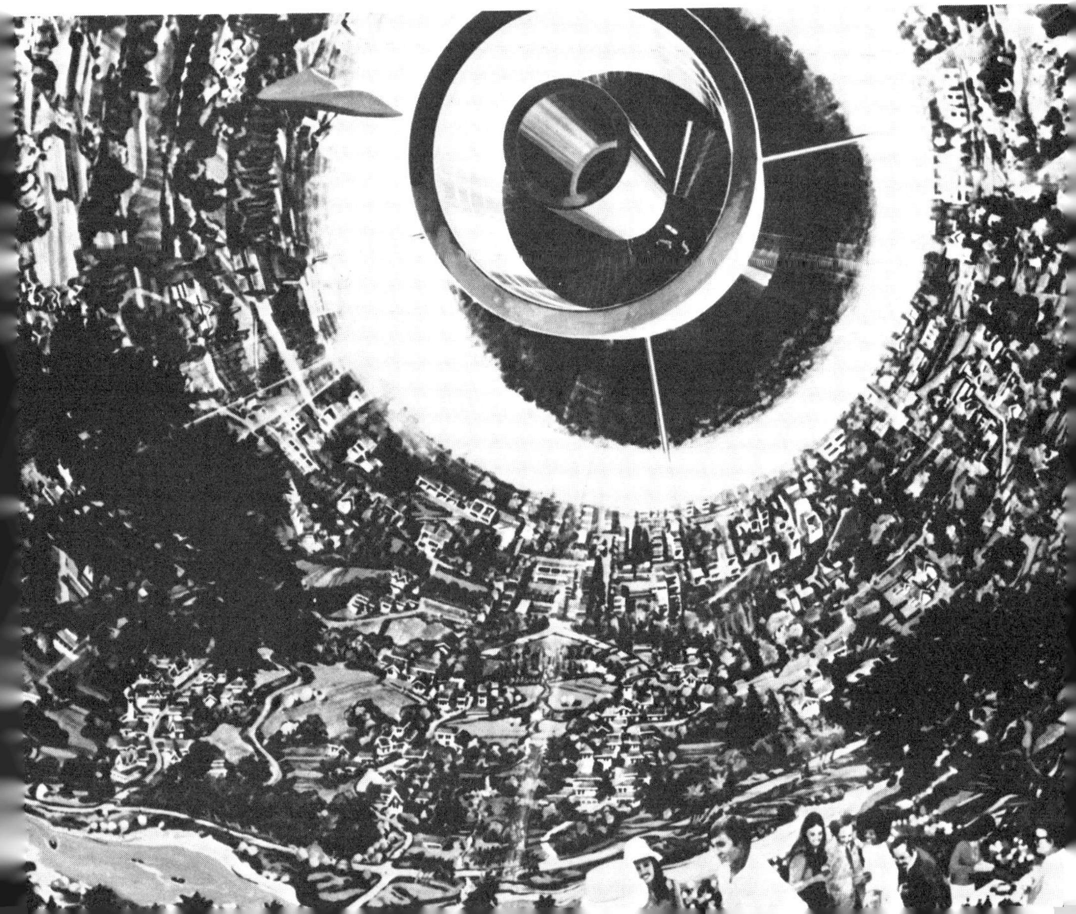

hundred such cylinders are mounted on a ring (a hollow curved tube) some 14 kilometers across. Most of them are used for farming—for raising crops and livestock. A few of them might house small factories.

The main factories, control centers, and docking ports are located at either end of the long cylinder. People enter and leave them through zero-gravity tubes.

Colonists can see clouds in their sky. The atmosphere is deep enough to cause light dispersion, so that the "sky" is blue. The atmosphere is also dense enough to cause collisions of cosmic particles, and these collisions remove much of the energy in the particles. A colonist looking into the sky can see the other residence strips far in the distance. But because of the distance and the clouds, details are not apparent.

People's living arrangements vary. Some colonists prefer to live in small villages of single-family houses. They may be clustered and the cluster surrounded by forests, lakes, and streams. Others prefer apartment living in the small cities that have been developed and in which businesses, museums, theaters, and sports centers are concentrated.

Very likely these gigantic colonies will be built in pairs. A major outing will be a visit to a sister colony, which might have sections for "weightless sports," or an area set aside for

Eventually there may be super colonies such as this, each some 25 kilometers long and 6 kilometers in diameter. The ring of smaller cylinders will be for farming and for small factories. Over a million people could live in such a colony.

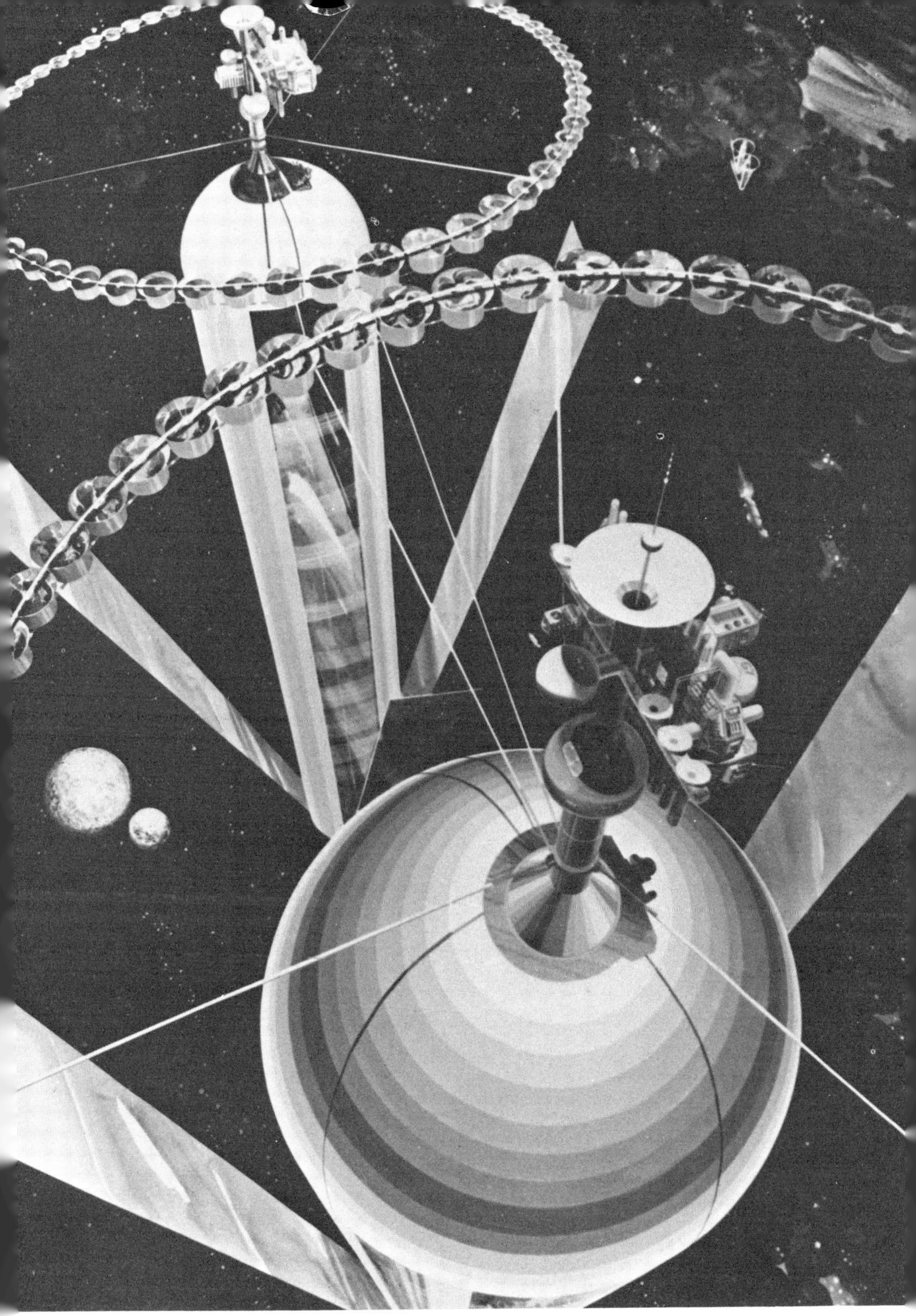

Inside Colony Four. Three strips of habitats stretching into the distance are separated by three strips built to admit sunshine.

winter activities, such as skiing, ice skating, or bobsledding. Journeys to other "worlds" would also be possible and practical—to the Moon and, on rare occasions, to Earth.

Mining the Asteroids

As we said before, the materials needed to construct colonies will at first have to come from Earth. As soon as possible, Moon mining will be developed as a source of raw

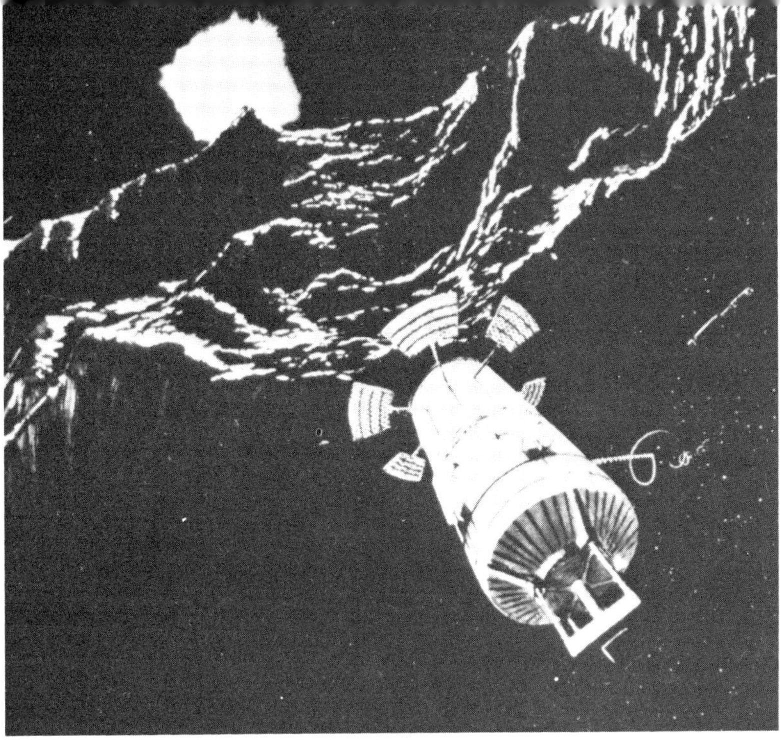
A spaceship closes in on an asteroid.

materials. However, as more advanced colonies are constructed, colonists will move out among the asteroids, seeking those that can be mined for raw materials.

At the American Museum of Natural History in New York City, there is an iron-nickel meteorite that weighs over 30 000 kilograms. It is probably a stray asteroid. The word *asteroid* means "starlike," so called because the objects look like dim stars when seen through a telescope. Asteroids are large chunks of metal (iron, for the most part) that move in orbits around the Sun. They range in size up to some 800 kilometers in diameter. There are thousands of them, perhaps millions, and they are concentrated in the region between the orbits of Mars and Jupiter.

Since asteroids are rich in metals, they are promising

sources of iron and other raw materials for future space colonies. An early project of the people in advanced colonies may be to design a research ship able to journey to the asteroid belt. Such a ship might support twenty or thirty engineers for a period of several years.

Engines for the ship need not be large and powerful, for they will always operate in zero gravity or very close to it. There is some gravity on an asteroid—how much depends on its mass—but even the largest ones have only a small fraction of the gravitation of Earth.

The ship's engines might be solar-powered. They might work by ejecting an exhaust of oxygen. The gas will be available, for lunar ores contain considerable oxygen. The ship's engines might also be mass-drivers that eject pellets of lunar slag.

In addition to the "iron asteroids," there may be others that have rich supplies of other materials. Occasionally meteorites containing large amounts of hydrogen, nitrogen, and carbon fall to Earth. These could be fragments of asteroids, as studies of the light reflected from certain asteroids indicate that these materials are present in them. They are the very materials that are lacking in lunar ores and that are essential to the space colony. It may be that the research ship will gather in those carbon-rich asteroids and transport them back to the space colony, which would make the colony completely independent of Earth.

Colonies Beyond the Asteroids

The asteroids probably contain all the material a colony needs, both for building and for life support. Therefore, it seems logical that colonies of the twenty-first or the twenty-second century will be constructed in the asteroid belt. They will be close to raw materials. They will also be close enough to the Sun to receive large amounts of energy.

Solar radiation drops rapidly with distance. However, distant colonies can gather the energy they need by using large mirrors. The boundary for solar-powered colonies is about 50 light-hours, ten times farther out than the orbit of Pluto. Beyond that distance, the size and mass of the collecting mirrors would have to be made too large to be practical. (A light-hour is the distance light travels in one hour, more than a billion kilometers.)

An asteroid colony, or one much farther out, even at the solar boundary, would remain in orbit forever, just as planets will. And since it will be able to get supplies of nitrogen, hydrogen, carbon, as well as other materials from the nearby asteroids, the colony will be completely self-contained.

As the population of a colony grows, there will be pressure for additional colonies. These will be built, but eventually the colonies must limit population growth to zero, or to a very low value—a fraction of a percentage point. This can be done by controlling the number of children allowed in the family. In that way, there will be abundant energy and material for everyone, and plenty of living space plus open areas.

Starship

People welcome new horizons. They are stimulated by new adventures and not content until they have explored

Eventually a starship built at Colony Three, or perhaps at Colony Four, will be launched into an orbit that will take it far beyond the solar system and out to the stars.

new challenges. And they are always curious. The early inhabitants will be in a colony for just such reasons. Once there, they will continue to expand to new worlds. The most challenging of all, and the one that has fascinated people for centuries, is the universe of stars.

Someday colonists will build a starship. It will take off from a colony and begin a journey to the stars. The journey will be everlasting, for the nearest star beyond the solar boundary is Proxima Centauri, over 4 light-years away—

over 30 000 000 000 000 kilometers. (If a starship could go 300 000 kilometers per second, which no spaceship can, it would take over four years to reach the star.) Most of the stars are much farther away.

Beyond the solar boundary some other kind of energy must be found to maintain the colony, to provide light and warmth and electric power. Nuclear energy has been suggested and may be used. However, it is more likely that some way of combining matter and antimatter will be developed. At this time we do not know how this can be done. But during the next century or so scientists will continue to search for ways to accomplish this.

Although the technology seems complicated, the idea is quite simple. For every positive thing in the universe, there is a negative. When the two combine, energy is released. For example, for electrons (which are negative) there are antielectrons, or positrons (which are positive); for protons there are antiprotons; and so for everything there is an opposite.

Conceivably, a starship could carry large containers of hydrogen (protons and electrons) and of antihydrogen (antiprotons and positrons). Let's imagine that, in some way not yet developed, the gases are fed into a reactor, where they annihilate each other. In the process, tremendous amounts of energy are released. This energy is harnessed to electric generators. In theory, it would be possible to carry enough reserves to provide energy for billions of years—certainly enough for a starship to search widely for life on a planet in orbit around a distant star.

Perhaps long before the starship eases into an orbit

around that far-off planet, people will have received radio signals from a world beyond our own. Starship One will provide us with our first view of that world. And people from that ship will be the first to meet face-to-face other creatures of the universe.

10

Can It Really Happen?

Throughout the history of mankind, people have been asking, "Can it really happen?" The question was asked when people first thought of going out on the oceans.

It was asked when Columbus set out on his journey, and as Marco Polo set sail. People thought the ships would drop off the edge of the world.

In the 1960's, when astronauts made plans to reach the Moon, many people believed it could never happen. But men did walk on the Moon, and they rode across the surface in Moon cars.

And what about space colonies? Can they really happen? The answer is a strong yes. Space colonies can be built. Right now engineers have the knowledge needed to get started.

Space colonization is in our future. It offers endless opportunities for people to expand. There are resources in space—endless energy, materials in the Moon and the asteroids, the advantages of weightlessness and a high vacuum.

The opening of the space frontier will be exciting. It will challenge the entire world. Each nation will be working on something outside its boundaries, and people from all corners of the world will be deeply involved in the most thrilling adventure that mankind has ever attempted.

Nations with the most advanced knowledge of electronics and the most industries will take the lead, but probably many countries will contribute scientists and engineers. Early space colonists will come from all over the world. Space colonies will bring people together for a great international effort. They may be a strong force for peace among all nations.

Life in a space colony should be very satisfying. People will have a high standard of living—a pleasant home, plenty of food, unlimited energy, and challenging opportunities.

Many people from Earth may prefer to live in space colonies, where the weather can be controlled, days can be made longer or shorter, and seasons can be adjusted to please the population. A person can be weightless, if desired, or live in a region where there is gravity, in surroundings more like those of Earth itself.

Each colony will have its own managers and engineers—people responsible for the operation of the colony. And each person will have a sense of responsibility, an essential part to play in the success of the colony.

The only certainty in the future is that radically new things will be happening. The only way to explore it is to use your imagination.

Further Reading

Chapman, C.R., "The Nature of Asteroids," *Scientific American* (January 1975), pp. 24–33.

Cooper, Henry S.F., *A House in Space.* New York: Holt, Rinehart and Winston, 1976.

Grey, Jerry and Christine Krop, eds. *Space Manufacturing 111.* New York: American Institute of Aeronautics and Astronautics, 1979.

Heppenheimer, T.A., *Colonies in Space.* New York: Warner Books, 1978.

NASA, *Space Colonization: A Design Study.* Washington, D.C.: U.S. Government Printing Office, 1978.

NASA, *Space Resources and Space Settlements.* Washington, D.C.: Scientific and Technical Information Branch, 1977.

O'Neill, Gerard K., *The High Frontier.* New York: William Morrow, 1977.

Ryan, Cornelius, ed., *Across the Space Frontier.* New York: Viking Press, 1952.

Index

About the Author

Franklyn M. Branley, Astronomer Emeritus and former Chairman of The American Museum–Hayden Planetarium, is well known as the author of many books about astronomy and other sciences for young people of all ages.

Dr. Branley holds degrees from New York University, Columbia University, and the State University of New York College at New Paltz. He and his wife live in Sag Harbor, New York.

Branley, Franklyn M.

Space colony: frontier of the 21st century